# American Ethnic Practices in the Twenty-first Century

# American Ethnic Practices in the Twenty-first Century

## *The Milwaukee Study*

Jill Florence Lackey

**LEXINGTON BOOKS**
*Lanham • Boulder • New York • Toronto • Plymouth, UK*

Published by Lexington Books
A wholly owned subsidiary of The Rowman & Littlefield Publishing Group, Inc.
4501 Forbes Boulevard, Suite 200, Lanham, Maryland 20706
www.rowman.com

10 Thornbury Road, Plymouth PL6 7PP, United Kingdom

British Library Cataloguing in Publication Information Available

**Library of Congress Cataloging-in-Publication Data**

Lackey, Jill Florence.
  American ethnic practices in the twenty-first century : the Milwaukee study / Jill
Florence Lackey.
     pages cm
Includes bibliographical references and index.
  ISBN 978-0-7391-7829-4 (cloth : alk. paper) — ISBN 978-0-7391-7830-0 (electronic)
1. Ethnicity—Wisconsin—Milwaukee—Case studies. 2. Ethnic groups—Wisconsin—
Milwaukee—Case studies. 3. Milwaukee (Wis.)—Ethnic relations—Case studies. 4.
Milwaukee (Wis.)—Social life and customs—Case studies. I. Title.
  GN560.U6L33 2013
  305.8009775'95—dc23                                                    2013017111

Printed in the United States of America

# Contents

Acknowledgments                                                      vii

1   Why Should We Care About Ethnicity?                              1
2   The Milwaukee Study: Its Methodology and Context                 9
3   Ethnic Practices: Organizations and Their Functions             21
4   Ethnic Practices: Language and Language Retention               33
5   Ethnic Practices: Ties to Past Homelands                        39
6   Ethnic Practices: Religion                                      43
7   Ethnic Practices: Food                                          51
8   Ethnic Practices: Art Forms                                     57
9   Ethnic Practices: Healthcare and Healing                        63
10  Ethnic Practices: Genealogy                                     69
11  Ethnic Practices: Political Activity                            75
12  Ethnic Practices: Working                                       81
13  The Sum of Ethnic Practices                                     93
14  Life in Multi-ethnic America                                    99
15  Threats to Ethnicity                                           119
16  A New Vision for American Ethnicity                            133

Appendix                                                           139
Bibliography                                                       143
Index                                                              153
About the Author                                                   157

# Acknowledgments

Between 2000 and the end of 2012, seventy anthropologists (including myself) and anthropology interns worked on this study, mainly as interviewers. The process was rigorous, yet fun. I will always recall the meetings we'd have in my apartment or at the Urban Anthropology office discussing and comparing our latest interviews. I think we were all startled to learn just how vibrant ethnicity still is in Milwaukee, and possibly beyond Milwaukee. I wish to thank these individuals: George Anachev, Ericka Bailey, Amanda Balistreri, Jill Barganz, Ole Bassen, Laurel Bieschke, Erin Bilyeu, Abena Ivory Black, Crystal Blair, Jaime Bodden, Sarah Bradley, Ed Bremberger, Annette Centenno, Stacey Cushenberry, Michelle Dekutowski, Katy Dineen, Kathrin Fiedler, Alejandra Estrin, Bix Firer, Laura Finley, Erinn Brittney Gedemer, Carolyn Hall, Amy Hilgendorf, Scott Hamann, Meghan Houlehen, Whitney Johnson, Tony Johnson, Lynn Johnston, Jessica Kegel, Nkosi Knight, Beth Krueger, Joe Kubisiak, Ayn Lee, Martha Leuthner, Erin Malcolm, Jeremy Mattson, Cloe McCabe, Aimee McGinty, Jamie Merkel, Denise Meyer, Rebecca Mueller, Sarah Munson, Brenda Nemetz, Kim Osborn, Danielle Paswaters, Rick Petrie, Brooke Phelps, Troy Potter, Sara Rich, Anna Reidy, Paul Rivas, Mary Roffers, Jason Scott, Kathrin Schmid, Lily Shapiro, Megan Sara Sharpless, Lisa Spencer, Amy Svinicki, Tracey Tessman, Mike Theis, Jeff Thomas, Alexandra Trumbull, Chanel Updyke, Jenna Valoe, Lauren Christine Walls, Ashley Widowski, Kelly Willis, Amanda Ybarra, and Natalie Ann Zitnak.

I would also like to extend special thanks to Roberta Estes for her wonderful knowledge of DNA research that she was willing to share.

# Chapter One
# Why Should We Care About Ethnicity?

For over a century, scholars have written about ethnic phenomena. Most summarized recent studies or ideas of other scholars, and concentrated on ways that ethnicity benefited or failed to benefit individuals. This book takes a different approach by presenting information through the voices of the actual study participants, and explaining how ethnicity benefits not just them, but the larger society as well.

Between 2000 and 2012 the research organization, Urban Anthropology Inc., conducted a qualitative study of ethnic groups in Milwaukee County. During this span, local anthropologists and anthropology interns interviewed 434 informants who were heavily involved in ethnic practices, and conducted observation at ethnic gatherings.

This study was limited to ethnic practices, experiences, and ideas in one Midwestern city. It did not expand into issues of race, class, or gender in Milwaukee or the United States, although the author recognizes the salience of these issues in American history and their interaction with ethnic interests and identity. The purpose of the study was to learn the potency of ethnicity in an urban area, gain an understanding of ethnic practices in the early twenty-first century, and find out what—if anything—local ethnic involvement contributes to the wider society. The strength of qualitative interviewing is that readers have the opportunity to discover some of the answers to these questions in the informants' own words.

But before the study and its findings are introduced, two questions will be addressed. How is ethnicity defined and why should we care about ethnicity at all?

## Defining Ethnicity

Over the years, social scientists have defined ethnicity in a variety of ways. As late as the 1970s ethnicity was often treated as a pejorative term used to single out anyone not Anglo-American (Hicks, 1977). For those objectively attempting

a definition, most appear to agree that ethnicity involves (a) biological connections (e.g., Narroll, 1964; Salter, 2002); (b) an orientation toward the past (e.g.,
Alba, 1990; Greeley, 1971); (c) subnational or subcultural status (e.g., Eller,
1999; Greeley, 1971; Tonkin, McDonald, & Chapman, 1989); (d) practices that
are shared and distinguishable, (e.g., Cohen, 1974b; Narroll, 1964); and (e) an
element of choice in identity and participation (e.g., De Vos, 1975; Espiritu,
2001; Waters, 1990).

Since Fredrik Barth wrote the introductory chapter to *Ethnic Groups and
Boundaries* in 1970, some social scientists—particularly sociocultural anthropologists—have challenged older definitions of ethnicity. Disputing the commonly held notion of the time that ethnicity is a static and lifelong attribute,
Barth saw ethnicity as situational with ever-changing boundaries. Anthony
Cohen (1994) found the concept of ethnicity vague, variously used, and objecti-
fying. More recently, Marcus Banks (1996, p. 190) suggested that ethnicity is as
much a creation of academics as it is a category used by those claiming it.

> Because of a constant conflation between description and explanation in folk
> theory, a conflation analogous to and perhaps derived from mumbo-jumbo aca-
> demic jargon, ethnicity is constantly produced as explanation: the reason why
> the A's are slaughtering the B's, the reason why the C's are "clannish", "dirty",
> or "unreliable" . . . [Ethnicity is] a collection of rather simplistic and obvious
> statements about boundaries, otherness, goals and achievements, being and
> identity, descent and classification, that has been constructed as much by the
> anthropologist as by the subject.

And how did the Milwaukee County informants understand ethnicity?
These informants, representing over sixty ethnic affiliations and over 250 ethnic
organizations in the urban area, had no difficulty whatsoever with the term. As
will be evident through the extensive use of quotations in this book, most believed an ethnic group has close or distant biological connections, ties to a past
geographical area, and shared practices. For purposes of clarity, this work will
use Alba's definition of ethnicity (1990) as it is closest to the informants' understanding and distinguishes it most clearly from other social categories. Hence,
ethnicity involves biological linkages, shared practices, an element of subjectivity, and unlike many other group memberships, "is oriented toward the past,
toward the history and origin of family, group, and nation" (p. 37).

Race, unlike ethnicity, does not necessarily involve biological connections
to the past. Schaefer (2007, p. 8) defines race as follows.

> The term *racial group* is reserved for minorities and the corresponding majori-
> ties that are socially set apart because of obvious physical differences. Notice
> the two critical words in the definition: *obvious* and *physical*. What is obvious?
> Hair color? Shape of an earlobe? Presence of body hair? To whom are these
> differences obvious, and why? Each society defines what it finds obvious.

Race is also a more unstable and mutable category than ethnicity and more likely to be assigned by outsiders than ethnicity (Jacobson, 1998). It is often used to subordinate some groups. For example, in the US, whiteness has been consistently privileged over non-whiteness. Race, thus, is a physical appearance that is often assigned in order to subordinate others and not to be confused with ethnicity.

But what are African Americans? Cornell & Hartmann (2007, p. 34) claim they can fit both categories of race and ethnicity.

> They are held by others and often by themselves to be members of a distinct race, identified primarily by skin color and other bodily features. At the same time, they have also become an ethnic group, a self-conscious population that defines itself partly in terms of common descent (Africa as homeland), a distinctive history (slavery in particular), and a broad set of cultural symbols (from language to expressive culture) that are held to capture much of the essence of their peoplehood. When they lay claim to an identity of their own making and meaning and when they act on the basis of that identity, they are acting as an ethnic group.

In the Milwaukee study, African American informants lay claim to this identity and are thus treated collectively as an ethnic group.

This book is about ethnicity. But a question remains: Why should we care at all?

# Why Ethnicity Matters

Ethnicity has often been represented in superficial ways in American popular culture. Consider the following example. As the Urban Anthropology ethnic study was winding down, a group of the organization's anthropology interns conducted an unscientific survey at a popular shopping mall. The survey was designed to give interns some insight into what Milwaukeeans knew about the contributions of ethnic practices to America. While some individuals, who were deeply involved in their ethnic groups, gave in-depth answers to the questions, most of the others knew very little. The following responses provided by a middle-aged European American woman were very typical of the forty-six people interviewed who lacked strong ties to their ethnic group.

> Intern: How many ethnic organizations do you think exist in Milwaukee?
> Woman: Uh, probably five. Ten?
> Intern: Would you be surprised to learn there are over 250?
> Woman: I'd be amazed. Where are they hiding?
> Intern: Do you think ethnic practices are good for America? By "practices" we mean the things that ethnic groups do that are tied to their heritage.
> Woman: Well, probably they are good. I mean, we are a nation of immigrants.

Intern: Can you state some specific ways that ethnic practices are good for
America?
Woman: [Pause.] Well, the food and restaurants, for sure. Chinese, Italian,
Mexican.
Intern: Anything else?
Woman: Maybe dress styles. The ethnic festivals.
Intern: Anything else?
Woman: [Pause.] Sorry, nothing more is coming to me.

The woman's responses reflect some of the better known ways that ethnic
practices contribute to the American way of life. But food and festivals comprise
the small picture. There is also a larger picture. In a multicultural environment,
ethnic groups extend their practices and the effects of the practices across other
collectivities, such as families and extended families, workplaces, neighborhoods, towns, and nations, and in the process, strengthen them on many levels.
As will be demonstrated through findings from the Milwaukee study, the practices build assets across other collectivities. In doing so, they help restore a balance between the focus on individualism and the focus on collectivism in the
United States.

## Individualism and Collectivism

The two concepts differ in significant ways. Individualism can be defined as a
social pattern where loosely-connected people view themselves as independent
of collectivities. Human beings are motivated by self-interest, rational decision
making, and goals that are often irrespective of the goals of others. On the other
hand, collectivism is a social pattern where loosely-connected people view
themselves as part of one or more collectivity and are motivated by the norms
of, and duties imposed by, those collectivities. Preserving and enhancing the
well-being of the group is a major guiding principle for social action (Ho, 1979,
p. 144; Triandis, 1995, p. 2).

There are arguments for the benefits and detriments of either individualism
or collectivism in the scholarly literature. For a nation, a focus on individualism
can result in a higher gross national product and fewer internal tensions resulting
from competing collectivities. For individuals, the focus can lead to greater economic resources, higher self-esteem, and more intellectual and entrepreneurial
freedom. However, individualism can also lead to loneliness, poor social support, and lack of shared behavioral codes. Conversely, a focus on collectivism
leads to a more orderly, more crime-free society due to controls from the social
environment. For individuals, a focus on collectivism can enhance stability and
group anchorage—an attribute particularly important in fulfilling youth identity
needs. However, collectivism can also result in overly compliant individuals or
development of extremist groups like criminal gangs or the Ku Klux Klan that

tend to be highly collective (Eibl-Eibesfeldt, 2004; Hirschfeld, 1996; Patterson, 1977; Triandis, 1995; Williams, 1964).

Few scholars claim that America has struck a balance between individualism and collectivism. Hofstede (1980) calls the United States the most individualistic nation on earth. According to Gellner (1995, p. 19), "America is inclined to culture-blindness because, on the whole, it takes its own luminously individualistic culture for granted and sees it as manifestly obvious."

The United States was founded on the principles of classical liberalism developed by the end of the eighteenth century, which included free markets, liberty of individuals, and freedoms of religion, speech, press, and assembly. American development of the frontier and capitalism enhanced this focus on liberalism and individualism. The demands of hard work, isolation of the frontier where behavioral codes from former homelands were forgotten, and the constant mobility of populations left many Americans developing their own morality (Brislin, 1981; Westen, 1985). With the frontier came the need for goods from the east coast which propelled more development, including railroads (Turner, 1958). In the capitalist mentality, states Rosenblatt (1999, p. 3), once Americans ran out of real frontier, "we made other things to not have," and went in pursuit of these. Classical liberalism evolved into neoliberalism by the late nineteenth century, with a stronger emphasis on laissez-faire economics and individuals who were now interpreted as "self-interested beings who seek material advancement, while rejecting public or social intervention into their lives" (Howard, 2007, p. 3). The individual was gradually conceptualized as the source of power and value that was once attributed to the group.

Perhaps it was this focus on the individual that influenced the way Western social scientists—particularly Americans—theorized ethnicity.

## Popular Theories on Ethnicity: Primordialist versus Instrumentalist

Since the 1970s, nearly every major publication on ethnicity has included the debate over the primordialist versus the instrumentalist view of ethnicity. While other theories did arise, none developed the following of these two approaches. Both views sought to explain why individuals retain loyalty to their ethnic groups.

According to the primordialist view, individuals have affective ties to their ethnic group (Levine, 1997). Early scholars conceptualized ethnic groups as discrete cultures rooted in shared biological origins—as associations of people with distinctive traits such as food, music, folklore, dialect, values, music, and beliefs (Narroll, 1964). The differences between ethnic groups were said to have developed because of geographical isolation where traits were cultivated and transmitted as part of the "intimate" culture experienced in childhood and through childrearing practices (Barth, 1970; Epstein, 1978). In the primordialist view, the attachments stem from the individual's sense of the "givens" of the cultural existence (Geertz, 1973; Novak, 1975). The most affective tie—loyalty—is a natural phenomenon realized through biological links. According to Van den Berghe (1986, p. 261) ethnicity is "clearly an extension of kinship, the addition of outer skins to the onion of nepotism. . . . Many contemporary African societies, despite their size and complexity, still project a clear image of ethnicity as a *nested* concept which shades into the clan, the lineage, the extended family, the nuclear family and ego." As long as biological existence has a value to the individual organism, ethnicity would persist (Hoddie, 2006; Shils, 1968). Because of the biological ties and the "natural" loyalty these ties engender, membership in an ethnic group remains permanent.

This loyalty was demonstrated in a study of World War II soldiers conducted by Shils (1957) who found that combat readiness and morale were more a function of personal attachments to families than patriotism and loyalty to the state—a finding he extended to ethnicity. Other scholars followed. Even as studies in the mid-twentieth century began to focus on cultural assimilation, some social scientists remained steadfast in their claims that kinship ties and shared practices resulted in a natural loyalty to ethnic groups. Greeley (1971, p. 186-187), in an attempt to modify the primordialist theory, argued that the ties were manifest in immigrant populations in the US.

> The ethnic group . . . came into existence precisely so that the primordial ties of the peasant commune would somehow or other be salvaged from the immigration experience. But because the primordial ties have been transmuted does not mean that they have been eliminated. They simply operate in a different context and perhaps in a different way. They are, according to this second model, every bit as decisive for human relationships as they were in the past.

Despite the often adamant claims of the primordialists, social scientists began doubting the natural centripetal pull of the ethnic group. As early as the 1950s, Marxists argued that ethnicity was simply false consciousness that masked class interests, and functionalists saw it as a survival of the pre-modern era that preceded modern trends toward achievement and universalism (Van den Berghe, 1981). One problem was that few social scientists had been studying ethnic groups in a plural society (Despres, 1975). Devons and Gluckman (1964) began critiquing the concept of ethnicity as a closed system, circumscribed from the whole of the host society.

Much changed with Fredrik Barth (1970). Studying the Pathans of western Pakistan and Afghanistan, he noted the ways that individuals changed ethnic groups or passed as a different ethnicity when in pluralist and competitive environments. Rather than looking at ethnic groups as discrete associations, he began focusing on changes at their boundaries. He critiqued the old view of ethnicity developing in isolation and saw the group as interactive, malleable, and composed of free-willed individuals strategizing for personal advantages. This was the beginning of the instrumentalist view of ethnicity and alternative motivations for maintaining loyalty to the ethnic group.

The instrumentalist approach that more or less began with Barth rarely addressed issues of common ancestry or diacritica such as language, food, dress, and ritual. The ethnic group itself means little. It shifts shape to meet the situational needs of its members (Glazer and Moynihan, 1970), much like Anderson's nations in *Imagined Communities* (1991). Its boundaries and meanings are negotiated by both in-group and out-group members through competition for resources (Hopper, 2003; Nagel, 1998). The focus is on how free-willed individuals use ethnic identity in an *instrumental* way to pursue their own ends (Karner, 2007) and how they use allies to compete more effectively in campaigns for land, employment, political power, educational opportunities, or entrepreneurial specializations. As such, the ethnic association becomes an interest group (A. Cohen, 1974a, p. 97): "Ethnicity is fundamentally a political phenomenon, as the symbols of the traditional culture are used as mechanisms for the articulation of political alignments. It is a type of informal interest grouping."

Both the primordialist and the instrumentalist approach have strong critics among today's social scientists—some arguing that the primordialist view was overly simplistic and others claiming the emphasis on ethnic boundaries went too far in ignoring cultural content (Cornell, 1996). But few theorists or their critics have directed their attention to ethnic practices and their effects on the wider society. In both the primordialist and the instrumentalist approach, the theories attempt to explain how ethnic groups meet individual needs—whether the needs are affective or opportunistic. These (and a few peripheral theories lacking a following) have focused on individual needs. As will be demonstrated in findings from the Milwaukee study, individuals strongly involved with their ethnic groups had *multiple* reasons for ethnic involvement, including affective and opportunistic motives. What has not been addressed is how the sum of these practices helps restore a balance between individualism and collectivism in America.

## The Following Chapter

Chapter 2 will discuss the Milwaukee study and its methodology, urban influences on ethnic change and continuity, and ways that Milwaukee compares to other US cities. Study findings will begin with chapter 3.

# Chapter Two
# The Milwaukee Study: Its Methodology and Context

Between 2000 and 2012, seventy anthropologists and anthropology interns working or volunteering for Urban Anthropology Inc. conducted interviews and observations for a study on ethnic practices in Milwaukee County, Wisconsin. The Milwaukee study was designed to explore the diversity and sum of ethnic practices in this Midwestern urban center and form generalizations about the practices. It was not intended to be a series of studies of specific ethnic groups or to make generalizations about any ethnic group.

## Study Participants

The study was comprehensive. A total of 434 informants were interviewed from over sixty ethnic groups (the full list of groups is in the appendix). Observation was also conducted at forty-five sites where ethnic activities were in progress. The geographic area was Milwaukee County, which includes the City of Milwaukee and its closest metropolitan suburbs. In fourteen cases, informants living within a few miles of Milwaukee County were included in the sample if they had lived most of their lives within Milwaukee County.

### Sampling and Recruitment

Sampling in the Milwaukee study was purposeful, designed "to permit inquiry into and an understanding of a phenomenon *in depth*" (Patton, 2002, p. 46). Purposeful, according to Spradley (1979, pp. 44-49), requires that the potential informant be thoroughly enculturated and currently involved in the subject matter under study. In ethnic terms, ideal informants in the Milwaukee study were those defined by Cornell and Hartmann (2007) as having "thick" ethnic ties. The authors, applying a constructionist approach similar to Nagel (1998) and Waters (1990), examined the ways that ethnicity and race change, and how the circumstances that the groups face lead to greater or less involvement. Where a great deal of social life and individual or collective action is organized around the ethnic tie, the tie is said to be "thick" (p. 76). The Milwaukee research team developed a checklist of ten practices (including items such as ethnic advocacy and visits to the former homeland) that would help identify strong ties for potential informants (see full checklist in the appendix). An eligible informant had to be involved in at least five of the ten listed practices to be considered strongly involved in his or her ethnic group.

In most cases, informant recruitment began with the ethnic organizations in Milwaukee County. Wherever possible, interviewers recruited the leaders and secured names of others deeply involved in the organization. Using a snowball approach, each person interviewed was asked to name someone else who was heavily engaged in ethnic practices, whether or not they belonged to an ethnic organization.

There were instances where the ethnic group had no formal organization as a starting point for recruitment. If the 2000 census indicated that there were residents citing that ethnic background as their first ancestry in Milwaukee County, the research team searched for restaurants, bars, and shops with that ethnicity in its description, for qualified informants. Where that failed, the team tried personal networks, universities, listservs, and social media. In a few cases no informants meeting the criteria for strong involvement in a group were located. For other potential informants, the response rate was excellent. While some failed to return repeated phone calls or emails to set up interviews, only four of those who were actually reached refused the interview.

Qualitative sampling is usually purposeful and thus not intended to be representative of a larger population in the strict quantitative sense, but the research team still had to make decisions about the number of informants to be selected in each ethnic group. Thus, using available demographic data for the year the study began, the principal investigator (and author of this book) made a list of ethnic groups, their Milwaukee County population in 2000 (1990 census was used in year 2000), and the suggested number of informants to be interviewed under each. Four levels emerged.

1. If the Milwaukee County ethnic population was larger than 80,000 (African Americans, Germans, Mexicans, and Poles), 30 to 45 informants were interviewed in each group.

2. If the Milwaukee County ethnic population was between 25,000 and 80,000 (Irish and Italians), 20 to 29 informants were interviewed in each group.

3. If the Milwaukee County ethnic population was between 10,000 and 24,999 (English, Jews, Hmong, Norwegians, and French), 10 to 19 informants were interviewed in each group.

4. If the Milwaukee County ethnic population was under 10,000 (all others), 0 (where none meeting the criteria could be located) to 9 informants were interviewed for each group. (Milwaukee County population sources: US Census Bu-

reau: 1990 & 2000 Census & 2000 American Community Survey—First Ancestry Reported; Sheskin, 1996).

The exception to the above list was the American Indian population in Milwaukee County. While their numbers comprised less than 1 percent of the total population, the principal investigator made the decision to oversample them (n=29) because of sharp diversities from tribe to tribe. Ultimately, the research team found potential informants from over twenty Indian groups, but the major nations living in Milwaukee County in 2000 were Ojibwe, Oneida, Potawatomi, Menomonie, and Stockbridge Munsee. Hence most selected informants came from these nations.

Anthropologists in the Milwaukee study also made an attempt to recruit a representative sample (just under half) of all informants from multi-ethnic, often transitioning, neighborhoods. The purpose was to compare informants' attitudes of other ethnic groups by the types of neighborhoods they lived in.

All informants were identified by the ethnic designation they preferred, which was not necessarily the designation used in the US census. For example, most North American Indians chose their tribal designation. Recent immigrants from Africa often preferred their ethnic over national designations (e.g., Ibo over Nigerian). An informant from Iraq chose to self-identify as Arab. The full list of informant ethnicities and their numbers, as well as the scheduling of interviews between 2000 and the end of 2012, can be seen in the appendix.

Demographic data were collected on informants' gender and age groups. The genders were nearly equally represented in the sample with 51 percent male and 49 percent female. Of the age groups, 10 percent of the sample was under age 25, 50 percent was age 26 to 55, and 40 percent was over age 55. The older bias in the sample was generally due to the following circumstances: (1) leaders of ethnic organizations (often the first of each ethnic group to be interviewed) were often retirees who had more available time than others for leadership roles; (2) those referring potential informants often selected people they perceived to have more cultural knowledge and experience, hence were more likely to be older; and (3) young people were often less involved in ethnic practices (see chapter 18). No other demographic data were collected.

## Informants with More Than One Ethnic Background

The constructionist approach to ethnicity (which from the view of the ethnic individuals emphasizes diverse ways they can relate to their ethnic groups) does not apply in all aspects to the Milwaukee sample because these informants were specifically selected due to their strong involvement in ethnic practices. But the approach fits them in one aspect—the voluntary nature of ethnic involvement. More than half the informants claimed two or more ethnic backgrounds. They selected the one or ones they wished to identify with, and the choice could change over years. See the example below from the Milwaukee study.

*Irish 162*: I took pride in being German for, oh, perhaps twenty years. I ate German food, spoke enough German to get by, celebrated October Fest, etcetera. When I got closer to my Irish grandfather I began to take an interest in Irish things too. Before long I began to see just about everything out of the Irish perspective, do everything that the other Irish did.

According to Waters (1990), most individuals with mixed ethnic backgrounds will identify with the patrilineal line because their fathers' surnames make it easier to trace ancestry. This was also true in the Milwaukee study. However, some informants were heavily involved in more than one ethnic background. Four in the Milwaukee sample were interviewed as informants from two ethnic backgrounds.

# Study Methods

The Milwaukee study employed research strategies that are commonly identified with the sub-discipline of cultural anthropology. This included an ethnographic approach to the study, and qualitative data collection (interviewing and observing) and analysis.

## Ethnographic Approach

Ethnography is a research approach that seeks to understand cultural phenomena in a holistic way. Spradley (1980, pp. 30-31) describes it well. Ethnography is "usually done with a single general problem in mind: to discover the cultural knowledge people are using to organize their behavior and interpret their experience. . . . Comprehensive ethnography seeks to document a total way of life." Classic ethnographies have included data on a cultural group's language, economic pursuits, political processes, spiritual beliefs, recreational activities, food, art forms, healing practices, games, ethos, social organization, history, adaptation to the environment, change, and more. Many, if not most, anthropologists have also historically taken the "emic" point of view when collecting data, which attempts to focus on insider accounts of beliefs and practices (Goodenough, 1970). This emic point of view was usually brought to light through interviews with cultural insiders and observation of daily practices, which were also the strategies in the Milwaukee study.

Tonkin, McDonald, and Chapman (1989) claim that *ethnicity* is a more or less perfect pursuit for this anthropological approach. Eriksen (2003) states that anthropologists' recent interest in ethnicity has been successful in showing cultures in flux, in process, and the complexity and sometimes ambiguity of a group's existence.

However, ethnography also has its critics (e.g., Said, 1978; Sardar, 1999). Over the years, many anthropologists began to rely heavily on observation as their main data collection strategy, which frequently resulted in lengthy summaries and classifications of what was observed, in final publications. This allowed for much interpretation and theorizing without original data through which readers could judge the soundness of the interpretation. According to Raymond Firth (1989, p. 48), observation turned into summaries "demands much selection, with possible bias." To avoid overinterpreting the findings without displaying the data, the research team in the Milwaukee study made the decision to collect data mainly through interviews and observation and also display the original data in any publications on the study whenever it was feasible. Hence this book is heavy in interview quotations.

## Interviews

Face-to-face, audio-recorded interviews were conducted with 413 informants. In twenty-one cases, the informants asked to fill out the interview guide on their own without the interview. Interview questions were posed on the informants' specific involvement and history of involvement in their ethnic groups, ethnic practices that were of greatest importance to them, how they or their ancestors came to the US and Milwaukee, what they liked and/or disliked about Milwaukee, and comparisons they observed between their ethnic group and other ethnic groups. Informants also responded to a series of questions about themselves and members of their ethnic group they knew well. Included in this series were questions on family lives, social organization, religious practices, economic ventures, political practices, leisure time activities, organizations, current movements, needs, strengths, leaders, contributions, and policies and/or historical circumstances that had most influenced them. The interview closed with an invitation to include any other information they thought important and a request for names of other strongly involved members of their ethnic group. Interviews lasted between forty-five minutes and two hours.

Interviewers were trained through an interview guide developed by Urban Anthropology Inc. The guide included instructions on asking follow-up questions, probing techniques, courtesy and patience with interviewees, and alternative interview techniques when collecting data through surveys and life histories. In nearly every case, each interviewer would work with only one ethnic group. In order to help the interviewers ask competent follow-up questions, each also received a packet of information on their ethnic group of focus. The Milwaukee study used German-, Russian-, and Spanish-speaking interviewers for recent immigrants from these ethnic groups. In some cases the interviewers conducted the interviews with recent immigrants (e.g., Burmese, Polish) through interpreters.

## Observation

While the principal investigator of the Milwaukee study had developed a pre-liminary schedule of activities to be observed, this was abandoned when it be-came apparent that the informants were offering their own invitations to events. The events ranged from organizational or club meetings, to spiritual outings, to lectures, to art exhibits, to feasts, to full-fledged festivals. In some cases the ob-server became a full participant in the event. For example, in one case the an-thropologist was invited to take part in a sweat lodge ceremony. In many other cases, the observer participated in ethnic feasts.

The principal investigator conducted most of the observations, using a field note journal. Notes from this journal appear throughout the pages of this book.

## Data Analysis and Confidentiality

Maintaining informant confidentiality and data analysis went hand in hand. In most cases, the principal investigator transcribed the interview tapes and field notes. The human subjects committee at Urban Anthropology Inc. had written the informed consent form for interviewees, which stated that all names and identifiers would be removed from any published works. As the research team got deeper into the study, they began to realize how tightly knit the ethnic com-munities were—tight enough that an informant might be recognized by fellow ethnics by any combination of club/organization, neighborhood, or institution mentioned in a quote or field note. Thus, during transcription, these identifiers were replaced with substitutes such as "[name]," "[organization]," "[street]." Audiotapes were destroyed after the transcriptions were proofread. To further protect confidentiality, each informant was also identified by an initial number, and when quotes were added to publications, the original numbers were scram-bled.

Also simultaneous with transcription was coding. The principal investigator used simple topical coding (Bernard, 2006, pp. 399-404), beginning early in the transcription process. A series of broad umbrella codes were developed, which ultimately became many of the chapter titles in this book, such as "religion," "working," and "art." As more transcriptions were completed, the umbrella codes were then subdivided. For example, under the umbrella code of working came the subcodes of "first immigrant/migrant generation," and "later genera-tions." Under each of these subcodes came "nature of work," "reasons for type of work," "societal influences on work," and "comments on work ethic." Ulti-mately 154 codes and sub-codes were generated from over six thousand pages of interview transcripts and 180 pages of transcribed field notes.

## Limitations

The research team in the Milwaukee study committed to displaying as many quotes and events in progress as possible in this book. However, what informants say may be subject to interpretation. There are essentially two issues here. First, two informants from the same ethnic group may experience their ethnic practices differently. As stated in the introduction to this chapter, the study was designed to explore the diversity and sum of ethnic practices in the Milwaukee area and form generalizations about these practices and was not intended to make generalizations about any ethnic group. What appears to be an "authentic" ethnic practice to one member of an ethnic group may not appear so to another. Ethnic groups (and their members) are multiplex and in constant flux. See the following case in point from one recent immigrant.

> *Polish 125*: When I came here from Poland, I was surprised to see so many mistakes made in Polish culture. I am seeing Christmas customs and someone who is Polish American will tell me that this is what they do on Christmas Eve. I am trying to tell them that this is really not a Polish Christmas Eve. I said that I just came from Poland a few years ago and this is not the way it is done in Poland.

Of course, what the Polish informant was not considering was change. It might be that the person being criticized brought a custom from Poland in 1880 that was practiced at the time. Those that remained in Poland may have gradually changed the custom in response to circumstances they faced in their environment, and those in the US may have changed the custom in response to American influences.

A second consideration is the validity of the historical information provided by informants. If they discussed a historical event, the research team made the effort to verify the information before including the quote in published material. But many events described were experiences limited to the informants' families and were unverifiable.

A final issue is representation. To what extent can findings from the Milwaukee study be generalized to ethnic practices nation-wide? While the study was designed to apply to Milwaukee County only, no doubt some readers will find practices representative of other American communities as well. The next section will compare the Milwaukee area (and urban centers in general) to other US areas, along the dimension of ethnicity.

## The Setting

This section will address two questions. First, does urban life change ethnic practices? Second, how does Milwaukee County compare to other urban centers in the US?

## Urbanism and Ethnicity

Urbanization was supposed to dilute ethnicity. According to Cornell and Hartmann (2007, p. 8), "the common assumption from the late 1940s to at least the early 1960s was that the diverse identities carried by peoples such as these would disappear . . . Urbanization would bring groups together in cities, where they would mingle, intermarry, and exchange ideas, losing touch with their regions of origin." This idea had been developed in part by sociologist Wirth (1938) and anthropologist Redfield (1941), who argued that city life led to disorganization, superficial relationships, and the breakdown of kinship. Lewis (1952) argued against these ideas. By focusing more on individuals and families than abstract communities in his research methodology, he claimed that primary relationships stayed strong in cities. Early in the twentieth century, census data showed segregated ethnic tracts, often in the "lowest grade" sections of the city where assimilation was not progressing (Warner and Srole, 1945; Lieberson, 1963). But ethnic solidarity was not necessarily the rule either. Newer arrivals—especially if they were seen as lower class—often led to backlashes by the more tenured members of the same ethnic group (Hannerz, 1974).

By the 1950s the ethnic census tracts were less homogeneous, but did that mean ethnicity was losing strength in these areas? Claude Fischer (1975) had a different conception of the influence of city life. He argued that urbanism changes people, but not in a disorganized way. In cities, primary relationships probably did weaken, but people tended to form more subcultures and more voluntary associations. It was these voluntary associations that gradually became the chief organizing units of ethnic groups.

And did ethnic groups lose touch with their regions of origin? Foster and Kemper (1974) said it was wrong to conceptualize cities as "bounded." As cases in point, Mayer (1961) and Little (1973, 1974) showed how some African ethnic groups in towns maintained their village ties. In the Milwaukee study, one of the strongest ethnic practices was "ties to former homelands."

*North American Indian Menomonie 182*: It's important for many Indian people as well as myself to keep the ties to the rez. People might work here in Milwaukee and maintain a household, yet go home to the rez in summers. It's having a home in two places.

*Polish 180*: In Milwaukee we developed so many organizations to support Poland—or what should have been Poland. We'd get together in little clubs and got very involved in international issues. We think we played a role in the rebirth of Poland.

To return to the original question: Does city living change ethnic practices? Members of the ethnic group may not live in segregated ethnic communities as they once did. They may intermingle and intermarry with people outside the ethnic group and as a result the number of people involved solidly in ethnic practices might diminish. But the proximity factor has gradually been replaced with development of clubs and organizations that focus on ethnic practices such as the heritage of their former homelands.

Ethnicity, as a result, became more voluntary.

## Is Milwaukee Unique?

Are there characteristics about the City of Milwaukee and its surrounding county that make it *more* or *less* friendly to ethnicity? This is a difficult question to answer. In many ways, Milwaukee County is a typical metropolitan area in the Midwest. The Midwest was home to Great Lakes and Plains Indians (among others), and most early European contact was through the French fur trade. Many of the urban areas developed around major waterways, facilitating trade and industrialization; most Midwest cities also suffered the effects of deindustrialization beginning in the late 1970s.

The City of Milwaukee, with its 2010 population of 594,833, can be compared to other large cities in the Midwest. According to the 2010 census, other Midwest cities with a population of over 400,000 include Chicago, Columbus, Detroit, Indianapolis, Kansas City, and Omaha. In looking at the 2010 Census and American Community Survey for the surrounding counties of these cities (or in the case of Kansas City, counties), they bear similarities in ethnic makeup. In nearly every surrounding county (or counties) where data were available, the largest ethnic populations included African Americans, Germans, Mexicans, and Poles—the same as Milwaukee. Populations of Irish, Italian, and English were also relatively large in the counties. Wayne County (Detroit) was unique with Arabs included in its largest six ethnic populations.

Milwaukee also has a fairly unique ethnic characteristic (shared to some extent with nearby Wausau, WI and St. Paul, MN). This is a population of over 14,000 Hmong—an ethnic group from Southeast Asia. During the Vietnam War, many Hmong living in Laos backed US military and intelligence forces. When the war ended in 1975, they faced genocide and many fled to refugee camps in Thailand. In December 1975, Congress approved the immigration of some Hmong to the United States under the "parole" power of the US Attorney General. While the Hmong originally settled in areas all over the country, they regrouped after a few years and ended up in just a few states, Wisconsin being one of them.

But are there social or historical factors that make Milwaukee County more or less friendly to ethnicity? Here scholars disagree. According to the Brookings Institution (Tolan and Glauber, 2010), the Milwaukee area is less than hospitable to *racial* diversity. A selected Milwaukee metro area ties with the Detroit and New York metro areas in being the most black/white segregated urban center of America's top 100 metro areas. Milwaukee was also ranked in the top ten metropolitan areas for segregation between Hispanics and whites. The Brookings study, based on the American Community Survey's five-year estimates representing 2005 through 2009 numbers, was called into question by several Milwaukee scholars from the University of Wisconsin-Milwaukee. The UW-M researchers questioned the methodology of declaring a neighborhood segregated when over half the population is African American but 30 to 40 percent is white. It should also be noted that the Brookings Institution's definition for the Milwaukee metropolitan area included four counties, not just Milwaukee County. However, field studies conducted by sociologist Devah Pager (Pager, 2007; Pate, 2011) point to racial discrimination in hiring practices in the City of Milwaukee. In some cases the studies show that local employers would hire a white worker with a criminal record before hiring an equally qualified black worker with no criminal record.

But not every scholar agrees that Milwaukee County is inhospitable to diversity. Focusing again on the City of Milwaukee, the area has some unique historical traits. While most Midwest cities were developed by Anglo Americans, Milwaukee was developed by ethnic Germans. Germans settled in the area which would become Milwaukee beginning in the 1830s. They built breweries, tanneries, printing and publishing businesses, machine shops, confectionaries, bakeries, and much more. Known for their architectural prowess, many of the buildings they designed still stand in the twenty-first century. By 1890, German language newspapers had twice the circulation of English language papers (Paradis, 2006). Milwaukee was known nationwide as the "German Athens." Lackey (2006) argues that even the successful Socialist movement in Milwaukee, which produced three mayors that governed over forty years, had German roots.

But did this early German presence have any effect on the lives and practices of other ethnic groups? John Gurda, author of seventeen books on Milwaukee history and its institutions, suggests it did. In *The Making of Milwaukee* (1999, p. 65), Gurda states the following:

> On a more subtle, even subliminal, level, it can be argued that the Germans made Milwaukee safe for ethnicity. The simple fact that a non-English-speaking group was the city's largest made it easier, relatively speaking, for later arrivals to resist the melting pot. Pressures to assimilate were always present, but they may have been weaker in Milwaukee than in cities with larger Anglo-Saxon populations. The Yankees were outnumbered; it was acceptable to be something else. Several generations later, ethnic food, ethnic dance, and ethnic festivals exert an attraction that often surprises newcomers. Milwaukee's lakefront festivals in particular—African, American Indian, Arabian, Asian, German, Irish, Italian, Mexican, Polish—are convincing displays of continuing ethnic vitality, together drawing nearly 600,000 patrons each summer.

Milwaukee is fairly typical of Midwestern cities in ethnic makeup and industrial history. Milwaukee has a robust ethnic history that continues into the twenty-first century. However, lacking current and comprehensive ethnic studies in similar metropolitan areas, there is no way to state with certainty that Milwaukee County creates an environment that is more hospitable or less hospitable to the practice of ethnicity.

Before proceeding into the chapters on ethnic practices—the subject of this book—one subject must be addressed.

# Special Issues Concerning African Americans and North American Indians

Two concerns should be raised when considering African Americans and North American Indians among the scores of other ethnic groups in the Milwaukee study. First, with a few exceptions, neither group came under Anglo American governance as voluntary immigrants. While some blacks did willingly emigrate from the Caribbean, South America, and Africa, most blacks were brought from Africa as slaves (D. Cohen, 1998; Waters, 1999). North American Indians, who were already in America when the Europeans arrived, were gradually stripped of their land and involuntarily fell under US authority. As non-immigrants, North American Indians and most African Americans did not approach US shores in hopes of new and better opportunities. Historically, their orientation toward American institutions was not that of other ethnic groups.

Second, although most ethnic groups experienced some effects of ethnocentrism and discrimination in America, none suffered like African Americans and North American Indians. Both groups had something the early European settlers wanted in order to develop and expand the American nation (Banton, 1983, p. 283).

> Whites treated Afro-Americans differently as a group because that way they could make more profit from the use of their labour power. They treated Native Americans differently as a group in the first place because they wanted the land which was the collective property of Indian nations, but in the second place because Native Americans appeared to have little contribution to make to economic development.

Both African Americans and North American Indians struggled to maintain remnants of their culture. During slavery, blacks were not allowed to speak in their native African tongues or maintain family ties. While a few scholars argue that some African traditions did survive slavery (e.g., Herskovitz, 1941), others claim that African culture was stripped from them, forcing blacks to develop new cultural forms during and after slavery (e.g., Frazier, 1939; Powdermaker, 1968). North American Indians were removed from their lands in the nineteenth century and corralled onto reservations. To eradicate their Indianness and isolate them from their collective identities and practices, the US government set policies such as the Civilization Regulations of 1880 that outlawed Indian religions and the General Allotment Act of 1887 that moved collectively held Indian lands into the hands of Indian families and individuals.

In addition, skin color and racial stereotypes set solid ethnic boundaries for African Americans and North American Indians. The phenotypical differences made both groups "unmeltable" during times when the melting pot was seen as the ideal goal of US ethnic groups (Eriksen, 2003). An African American could have one to three European grandparents and was still designated by outsiders as African American. Stereotypes intensified prejudice. Blacks were often portrayed in the popular media as mentally incompetent or criminal, while Indians were portrayed as warriors, victims, or artifacts (Peroff, 2001).

The bottom line is that both African Americans and North American Indians historically lacked the choices that other ethnic groups enjoyed—the choice to choose America and its institutions, the choice to practice their historic traditions, the choice to assimilate, and in some cases the choice to choose from mixed ethnic backgrounds. For all these reasons and more, one would expect African American and American Indian expressions about their practices, ideas, and aspirations to differ significantly from those of all others. In a few cases readers of this book will notice that this is the case. But the surprising finding in the Milwaukee study is that in most cases it is not.

## The Following Chapters

The remaining chapters will present findings from the Milwaukee study. Chapters 3 through 13 will discuss ethnic practices, beginning with the functions of ethnic organizations the Milwaukee informants discussed. The chapters that follow will summarize the ethnic groups' ties to past homelands, religion, food, art forms, healthcare and healing, genealogy, political practices, and economic activities.

# Chapter Three
# Ethnic Practices: Organizations and Their Functions

Much of the literature of the last fifty years has focused on ways that ethnicity gradually lost significance to individuals. According to the social scientists, this happened in part because groups were no longer segregated in ethnic enclaves where individuals were socialized in culturally specific practices (Yancey, Ericksen, and Juliani, 1976), and in part because individuals increasingly were products of multi-ethnic ancestry, leading to ambiguous identities (Gordon, 1964). While all this was true, the centrifugal push often added to the appeal of ethnicity. As more people had mixed backgrounds, ethnicity was becoming more subjective and voluntary (Waters, 1990). An individual could decide to identify with an ethnic background that was currently more popular or a better fit for one's personality. Personal passions such as opera and pasta could now be combined with affective ties (Alba, 1985; Bell, 1975). The significance of this voluntarism was consistently evident in studies where curious grandchildren were shown to be more likely than their parents to develop an interest in the cultural practices of their immigrant grandparents (Hansen, 1952).

As accentuated in chapter 2, all of the participants in the Milwaukee study were routinely involved in ethnic practices. This involvement was not the symbolic ethnicity of Herbert Gans, where nostalgic allegiance to the old country and pride in a tradition alone replaced face-to-face relationships in ethnic activities (Gans, 1979; Levine, 1997). Nor were the participants in this study limited to a particular social stratum, as had been predicted by Steinberg (2001). Groups at the bottom of the economic ladder were just as active in creating ethnic organizations and events as those at the top.

This chapter will focus on ethnic organizations.

## Membership in Ethnic Organizations

In the early nineteenth century, Alexis de Tocqueville (2000) maintained that voluntary associations kept Americans from excessive individualism. The process of organizing to accomplish mutual aims slowed the atomization and isolation processes that the author saw happening in the United States. He claimed that on the one hand voluntary associations helped extend equality to all citizens by giving them opportunities to be constructive participants and on the other hand promoted causes that were beneficial to the collective good of American society.

Voluntary associations have long been a vehicle for keeping ethnicity alive in the United States. In the early twentieth century, Robert E. Park pondered the paradox of how immigrants left undesirable conditions in their homelands only to enter a new world that gave them the chance to celebrate their past practices through ethnic organizations (Lal, 1990). Over the decades, the organizations have done more than focus on the past, as they've helped groups stay in touch and provided tangible political and economic benefits to members (Friedl and Chrisman, 1975; Lewis, 1974).

# Functions of Milwaukee Ethnic Organizations

In the Milwaukee study, participants described the efforts of over 250 ethnic voluntary associations in Milwaukee County. Nearly every ethnic group had at least one organization and some had over twenty—all of varying sizes and resources. A few were large-budgeted nonprofits with over one hundred paid employees, but most were small clubs funded through private donations and run by volunteers.

The organizations accomplished a myriad of functions for their members, from ethnic advocacy to festivals to media.

## Ethnic Advocacy and Anti-discrimination

Some organizations were founded with the goal of protecting members from violent attacks by people of prejudice. Others began in order to promote more positive cultural images. According to those interviewed, ethnic organizations in Milwaukee County having advocacy as one of their functions include those of the Slovenians, Palestinians, Chinese, Jews, Arabs, Taiwanese, Greeks, Scots, Norwegians, Italians, North American Indians, French, African Americans, Hmong, Mexicans, Puerto Ricans, Central and South Americans, and Irish.

> *Greek 153*: I am in [name of organization]. That organization was founded in 1922 in Atlanta. . . . It was formed in response to the persecution by the KKK in 1922 of Greeks in Atlanta, Georgia. They promote assimilation within American

society while promoting Hellenism, philanthropy, education, and personal responsibility.

*Irish 104*: The [name of organization] was organized to protect Irish Catholics even before the famine. This was during the days of "no Irish, no Catholics need apply." We protected the priests and the churches. Today we have various functions and fortunately don't need to spend much time protecting our Irish American citizens.

## Economic Support

Some ethnic organizations provide work opportunities, assistance to businesses, and job training. Some are professional associations. Others offer insurance, loans, and mutual aid. According to those interviewed, ethnic organizations in Milwaukee County having economic assistance as one of their functions include those of the Slovenians, Filipinos, Greeks, Norwegians, Irish, Central and South Americans, Italians, North American Indians, Jews, African Americans, Poles, Hmong, Mexicans, and Puerto Ricans.

*Salvadorian 110*: We have [name of organization] that helps us get training and find jobs. They work with employers and offer us cheap legal services on immigration issues.

*Polish 141*: The Polish federations. You purchased life insurance from the federation, and the salesman was part of [the] community. They had picnics, dances, programs, Christmas parties. In those days you worked at hard jobs and needed some kind of insurance if something went wrong, so the local fraternals were formed by the Poles. Today some of these fraternals still exist. They still offer insurance and help and still are social organizations.

## Political Support

Some ethnic associations assist members by organizing for political power in America and others advocate for policies that assist their groups' past homelands. According to those interviewed, ethnic organizations in Milwaukee County having political functions include those of the Arabs, Chinese, Palestinians, Slovenians, Irish, Greeks, Germans, Italians, Jews, North American Indians, Central and South Americans, Mexicans, Puerto Ricans, African Americans, Africans, Poles, Hmong, and Irish.

*Irish 166*: Historically, the Irish have been stronger in politics than any other group. Even today, when you look at who runs for office or who heads political departments, you will see a lot of Irish names. Traditionally the taverns were where we'd meet to discuss politics and decide who would run for what office.

But places like the [name of organization] also keep close tabs on what's going on in Ireland, and some of us play advocacy roles.

*African American 176*: It seems like all of our organizations have been pushing to get out the vote—on almost anything. There's always some voter registration drive going on for everyone or some push to vote in some election. But things aren't as clear as they once were. We say we have no power so we have to be better voters, but it's less clear nowadays as to who represents our interests, or even what those interests are. I even met some blacks that are against Obama for some reason or another.

*Mexican 144*: We have [name of organization] that works on immigration issues. We have a march once a year where we ask Latinos all over the city to take a vacation day from work and join us. We call this the "Day without Latinos," and it just shows how valuable we are by not being on the job for one day.

## Social Organization/Family Services

Many ethnic groups in Milwaukee County have organizations that focus on social organization—which can be families, extended families, lineages, or clans. Many of these organizations are helping people cope with changes in family practices and structure. According to those interviewed, ethnic organizations in Milwaukee County having social organization functions include those of the Slovenians, Palestinians, North American Indians, Italians, Arabs, African American Muslims, Puerto Ricans, Latvians, Irish, Jews, African Americans, Central and South Americans, and Mexicans.

*Hmong 125*: Our organization was always the clan system. The government did not provide funds for us. Divorce is done today too in the clan system. We have a judge. [We] go to that person. The person doesn't get paid. It's a social obligation. We also have [name of association] that has youth programs and family services. We still have early marriages at fourteen and fifteen and are trying to change this. But we are worried that the family does not work together as a unit anymore and creates imbalance in family. Kids are influenced by outside things. We help women and men to understand the roles they play. Women are becoming more self-reliant and sometimes seen as a threat.

*Jewish 145*: We have a family service organization. It used to be a relief agency for mainly immigrants in the 1800s and just evolved. When the Holocaust survivors came to America, they helped them get established. That's when the focus became families and children. Today there's a lot of focus on kids with parents separated or divorced, domestic violence, and kids' programs—especially when the parents work.

## Gender-specific Programs

Some ethnic organizations started out as women's or men's clubs, designed around the customary roles of men and women of the times. Over the decades some of the organizations became coed and some of the men's organizations spun off women's chapters. Others found more topical ways to attract only one gender. According to those interviewed, ethnic organizations in Milwaukee County having gender-specific functions include those of the Italians, African Americans, Greeks, Slovenians, Germans, North American Indians, Poles, Hmong, Puerto Ricans, Jews, Irish, and Mexicans.

> *African American 105*: My mother belonged to [name of woman's organization]. They made crafts for the folk fairs, like Raggedy Ann dolls and stuffed animals. They gave away the proceeds to support the vets and for scholarships for African American youth. I belonged to [another women's club] where we brought in dignitaries to speak and had teas. I also belonged to [another women's club] where they had seminars on race—people like Dr. Benjamin Mays, and others. We had "Monday after Easter" teas and had speakers at these teas.

> *Italian 142*: Then there is another group, which I belong to which is [name of women's organization]. It started out as a men's group. We are an offshoot, and our purpose is to provide service and scholarship. So we don't use the money for ourselves. Our group is not affiliated with the church or anything. Most of us are Catholic, but that is beside the point. That's not the purpose. I think we gave out—between the men's group and ours—we gave out eighteen $1,000 scholarships. You have to be part Italian, which is one of the requirements.

> *African American 108*: I belong to [name of men's organization]. It is designed to create positive black male development. There have been so many issues with black males not helping their children or being unemployed that someone has to step up and help. This organization is using responsible black men to mentor children and to help families succeed.

## New Settlers' Assistance

Some organizations help establish new arrivals in the Milwaukee County area. A few of the contemporary organizations had their roots in new settlement functions, but moved on to other services once the group was established. According to those interviewed, ethnic organizations in Milwaukee County having settlement functions *today* include those of the Central and South Americans, Chinese, Slovenians, Taiwanese, Filipinos, Italians, Burmese, North American Indians, Mexicans, Jews, African Americans, Africans, Russians, Poles, Hmong, and Puerto Ricans.

*Slovenian 155*: The difference between the [name of organization] members and other Slovenians is that the [organization] members were more recent immigrants, spoke the language natively, and had firsthand experience of growing up in the old country. Other Slovenians in Milwaukee are descended from earlier migrations and had fraternal life insurance or mutual aid organizations such as [names of organizations] organized into lodges that sponsored activities like bowling and social events. Those differences are blurring, now that [first organization] is increasingly second generation, too.

*Mexican 114*: [Name] is a Latino organization that is headquartered here in Milwaukee, but operates in other geographic areas as well. Mainly they help migrants in this area to become stable, get jobs, and other needed services.

## Leisure Time Activities

Many ethnic associations organize dances, parties, dinners, and picnics. Often these affairs are also ways to acknowledge contributing members of their group, as well as simply getting people together. In nearly every case, members of the wider population are invited to these functions too. According to those interviewed, ethnic organizations in Milwaukee County having leisure time functions include those of the African American Muslims, Palestinians, Arabs, Slovenians, Czechs, Slovaks, Chinese, Taiwanese, Filipinos, Irish, Greeks, Scots, Norwegians, English, Swedes, Germans, North American Indians, African Americans, Africans, Jews, French, Russians, Poles, Hmong, Kashubes, Mexicans, Puerto Ricans, and Central and South Americans.

*North American Indian Ojibwe 199*: Our organization puts on a huge event every summer at the lakefront. We attract thousands and the main event is a powwow. Indian dancers come from all over the state to perform and we invite the general public to dance with us too. At powwows there is never alcohol allowed. It's a celebration for the entire family and the entire community.

*Irish 120*: One of our events is the annual spaghetti dinner—not exactly an Irish entree, but, hey, it's easy to make for large crowds, which we get. It's held in the old neighborhood at [name of church]. It usually starts out with a mass. Then all come for the food. You never know what you're going to get. There used to be a cook, [name], whose specialty was brown spaghetti. No one knew if they should actually take the chance and eat the stuff.

## Educational Programs

Some ethnic organizations specialize in enrichment practices that educate their members, offering programs in past homeland language, history, travel, and current events. Some also provide college scholarships to members and others have their own schools that attract students from other ethnic groups as well.

According to those interviewed, ethnic organizations in Milwaukee County having educational functions include those of the Russians, Poles, Hmong, Slovenians, Chinese, Czechs, Slovaks, Scots, Greeks, Norwegians, Swedes, Germans, North American Indians, Jews, French, African Americans, Africans, and Mexicans.

*Italian 124*: The [organizational center] happens to be the largest facility of its kind in North America. It was built some twenty-five years ago with money raised by the Italian immigrants in Southeastern Wisconsin—primarily the Milwaukee area. A majority—some 80 percent of the Italians in Southeastern Wisconsin—are of Sicilian origin and a vast number of those reside in Milwaukee. The [organization's] goal is to promote our heritage and to work with the community on various types of programs, but basically it's to promote our heritage and our culture. We have enrichment programs in music, lectures, history, culinary arts there.

*Jewish 130*: The school was founded over a decade ago. About half a day is spent on Jewish studies and half on standard curricula. But our test scores, when compared to the secular schools, are outstanding.

*German 121*: In terms of the [name of organization], we think that we are the German response for the call for diversity and the perpetuation of it. We are very broad in our programming. Our aim is to perpetuate all forms of the German culture—the culture of German speaking communities. That encompasses parts of Switzerland, parts of northern Italy, Austria, Luxembourg, parts of eastern France, parts of western Poland. It's about the culture of the German language.

*Lithuanian 199*: This is the third school year that the [Lithuanian school] is open and running. It is a place for children and the new generation can learn about Lithuanian history, culture, and language. In my opinion, it's very important to know your ancestral roots, to live and move on, and accomplish new things in the future.

## Arts

Some organizations promote ethnic arts. This can include literature, and visual, performance, and culinary arts. According to those interviewed, ethnic organizations in Milwaukee County having art functions include those of the Central and South Americans, Greeks, English, Slovenians, Serbs, Norwegians, Swedes, Czechs, Slovaks, Italians, North American Indians, Jews, French, Poles, Hmong, Puerto Ricans, African Americans, Africans, Latvians, Irish, Mexicans, and Russians.

*Venezuelan 125*: At [name of organization], we do this by presenting artists of the different disciplines—dancing, visual arts, and literature. We also do educational programming by creating the possibilities of the different disciplines that instructors teach. We have folkloric dance, modern dance, ceramics, and we try to expand on those as well as formulize them. We also have a class for stringed instruments. We try to build a core group that can receive Latino arts, so they have the ability to do them and showcase it. It's offered to all. We target all, but we do have a special focus on educational groups and institutions—middle schools, grade schools, high schools, and college. We try to plant the seed for the growing population, so they learn how to appreciate Latino art.

*Italian 142*: I show them how to make pasta and let the children actually knead the dough. We teach them how to appreciate Italian culinary . . . and then they wind up with a spaghetti and meatball luncheon with milk, and water of course, and Italian bread and butter. We don't give them paper napkins, we give them cloth napkins, cloth tablecloth, and the water is in glass stemware.

## Charitable Causes

While most ethnic organizations support charitable causes for their own cultural group, some also support charitable causes of the general citizenry locally and worldwide. According to those interviewed, ethnic organizations in Milwaukee County having general charitable functions include those of the North American Indians, Arabs, Greeks, Slovenians, Scots, Jews, Poles, and African Americans.

*Palestinian 122*: I'll cite a couple of big examples. When the [2004] tsunami took place, I remember the [ethnic center] was raising money on a weekly basis to send to the tsunami victims. One particular service, for Hurricane Katrina, [name of person] said "I wasn't going to ask, but in five minutes I want to raise 250,000 dollars." And he did it. He raised 250,000 dollars from the congregation that was there at the time. A congregation of maybe around one thousand, maybe less. For Katrina also, we sent delegations from Milwaukee. We have a lot of doctors. They went down there with money, with medicine. We set up clinics, and gave out money. Different food and stuff like that. I think that sense of community has gone beyond our community.

*Jewish 121*: Traditionally, we've given to charitable causes that are not just Jewish or Israeli. We've had foundations that support causes of the general citizenry. One woman, who was actually a German Russian who had converted to Judaism, founded one of the largest foundations in Milwaukee, the [Name] Foundation. They give, not just to Jewish and Israeli causes, but mostly to the underprivileged and community causes.

## Sports and Gymnastic Programs

Some ethnic organizations sponsor sports leagues and ethnic games. Others have fitness functions that serve the wider society. According to those interviewed, ethnic organizations in Milwaukee County having sports and gymnastic functions include those of the Mexicans, Puerto Ricans, Scots, Italians, Czechs, Slovaks, Norwegians, Italians, Germans, North American Indians, Poles, Serbs, and African Americans.

*Puerto Rican 110*: I was in a little league named after Felix Mantilla who used to play for the [Milwaukee] Braves. It was run through the [name of organization]. Baseball was more of a Puerto Rican thing, and soccer was more the game of the other Hispanics, but there were a lot of Mexican kids in the league too.

*German 113*: Nature groups. There used to be a nature club in Milwaukee. We are members of [name of organization], which is really a health spa here in Wisconsin. The Germans have a history of being involved in healthy activities, with the nature walks and the gymnastics with the Milwaukee [name of organization].

*Scottish 130*: We have an annual highland games festival. It's more than the games, because we have food and music and sheepdogs, but our games are the big draw for Milwaukeeans. We boast athletic feats like the hammer throw and the standing heavy stone putt, 28 pounds.

*North American Indian Oneida 144*: I used to play lacrosse with the [name of organization]. It's played with a ball and a stick and you have to get the ball into the opponent's goal. Lacrosse is a traditional game among our people. It was outlawed for years because someone in government thought it had something to do with paganism. It's really popular now.

## Street Processions

A number of ethnic associations organize street processions or parades. Some of the events combine religion and ethnicity, and most plan the processions on special days of the ethnic group, such as St. Patrick's Day, *Dia de los Muertos*, or Juneteenth Day. According to those interviewed, ethnic organizations in Milwaukee County having street procession functions include those of the Mexicans, Italians, Poles, African Americans, Irish, and Scots.

*Polish 159*: Polish Constitution Day is May 3rd. It's about when the first Polish constitution was ratified in 1791. One of the organizations usually plans a procession at some auspicious place, like the monument to General Kosciuszko. The procession can be miles long or just a few blocks, depending on the era or the resources. Most of the time there is some kind of Polish band, a lot of banners and flags, people in Polish dress, and a really large group of people.

*Irish 155*: We have one of the few parades left in the city—our annual St. Patrick's Day Parade. We also have bands and dancers and our Shamrock Pipers that lead processions for all kinds of events. The Scots and Scots Irish participate and some others too.

*Norwegian 122*: We're in the St. Patrick's Day parade because Vikings invaded Ireland so they invite us to participate here in Milwaukee.

## Festivals

Far grander than parades and street processions are the festivals. Ethnic festivals can last for days and usually include food, crafts, entertainment, book-signings, celebrity appearances, processions, art forms, and genealogy tents. As Milwaukee is often called "the City of Festivals," there is hardly an active ethnic group that does not have one. They attract thousands of Milwaukeeans. According to those interviewed, ethnic organizations in Milwaukee County having festival functions include those of the Greeks, Serbs, Arabs, Chinese, Jews, Italians, Germans, African Americans, Africans, North American Indians, French, Poles, Hmong, Asians (collectively), Norwegians, Latvians, Mexicans, Scots, and Irish.

> *Italian 135*: As a matter of fact, we were the ones who started the ethnic council that brought together the presidents of all the ethnic festivals and we handle complex problems. We are very proud of the fact that we were the incubator for that kind of work. Festa Italiana started in the Third Ward before we had all the ethnic festivals on the Summerfest grounds. Today at Festa you'd get some of the best music, food, dancing, live performances, and kids' programs you can find in the country.

> *African American 166*: We have two annual festivals—African World Festival and Juneteenth Day. African World Festival is held at the lakefront and is about Africans everywhere. Because of its location you get a good number of whites attending. But Juneteenth Day is really our day—the day of African Americans. It's not just that it celebrates the end of slavery. It's in our neighborhood and it is really our culture here in America. It's not as glitzy, but it is packed. You get the best food and you see everyone you know.

## Healthcare Programs

Many of the largest medical centers in Milwaukee and in the United States In the early nineteenth century, Alexis de Tocqueville (2000) maintained were once started by ethnic groups. Over the years, most of these were taken over by nonprofit organizations or larger healthcare networks. According to those interviewed, ethnic organizations in Milwaukee County having healthcare functions *today* include those of the North American Indians, African Americans, and Latinos (combined backgrounds).

> *North American Indian Stockbridge Munsee 191*: Throughout our history here in the city there have always been those that organized to better our health. Whether

it's been treatment for diabetes, or alcohol abuse, or nutrition, we've had organizations like the [names of health centers].

*African American 111*: There are a number of issues that affect blacks more than other groups. One is access to healthcare. Others are tobacco use, HIV/AIDS, teen pregnancy and pediatric care, and mental health. The [name of organization] attempts to address these issues and empower African Americans with knowledge and resources to act as their own health advocates.

## Media

New immigrant groups have often been successful in founding bilingual newspapers and other media that keep ethnics informed of issues in both the new and old homelands. Some of these media gradually disappear when the group is more assimilated. According to those interviewed, ethnic organizations in Milwaukee County having media functions *today* include those of the Italians, Jews, African Americans, Hmong, and Latinos (collectively).

*Jewish 137*: We're a small community in Milwaukee and getting smaller, but we've never lacked for communication. Perhaps it is because we are so small. We've always had a Jewish newspaper or two in Milwaukee. The [name of newspaper] has been in circulation since the 1920s.

*Hmong 115*: We host a radio show to try and maintain the culture and speak the Hmong language on the radio. It has an international focus in Laos and Thailand.

## The Following Chapters

Clearly a plethora of activities are carried out by the ethnic organizations in Milwaukee. However, not all ethnic practices are performed within ethnic organizations. Most practices are carried out in families and informal groups. Chapters 4 through 12, which are intended to be encyclopedic, will describe the various practices that participants in the Milwaukee study observe, not just in the ethnic organizations, but in families and other settings that help them retain their ethnic identities. Ultimately these practices add assets to collectivities. Practices include language and language retention, ties to past homelands, religion, food, art forms, genealogy, healthcare and healing, politics, and working.

# Chapter Four
# Ethnic Practices: Language and Language Retention

Language is an all-important carrier of ethnic identity. According to Heller (1987), parents that want their children to maintain their culture must insist that the children speak the language. Often immigrants entered the United States speaking several languages from their homeland and surrounding areas (Whiteley, 2004). This was particularly true of the more recent immigrants in Milwaukee, where, for example, two Tanzanian Kuria claimed fluency in five languages, a Congolese spoke seven languages, and several Hmong and a Turk conversed in four languages.

In many countries—not just the United States—early immigrants lost their original languages unless the group had a large influx of new speakers (Lieberson, 1970). However, because the United States is a relatively homogeneous nation linguistically, immigrants were under greater stress to speak only English (Yinger, 1994). Participants in the Milwaukee study discussed their strategies for retaining, and sometimes relearning, the languages of their past homelands.

In order to access recent immigrants, the Milwaukee study used German-, Russian-, and Spanish-speaking interviewers from these ethnic groups. In some cases (e.g., Burmese, Polish) the interviews were conducted through interpreters.

## Retaining the Language

Nearly every participant in the Milwaukee study discussed the importance of language preservation to their group. See examples below.

*French 131*: If there is any engagement of policy [around French culture] it should be to try to save the French language in schools. Because I think more than thirty-three schools are eliminating the French programs, which I think is going to make the French studies very small. If the elementary schools stop teaching French, then the high schools will stop teaching French, and then nobody will be learning French anymore.

*Puerto Rican 104*: The language [is most important], because it unites us all, even though there are different dialects. I teach Spanish to my goddaughters, because their parents hardly speak Spanish at home, and I think it needs to be their primary language.

*Italian 130*: We had to keep some ties with Italy, and that was to talk Italian at home with the children. Our daughter who is married to a British man speaks Italian to her children. They understand almost everything. They don't answer all the time because their father speaks English of course. Culturally, it's to keep the language.

*North American Indian Ho Chunk 111*: The most important thing to me, for sure, is working on the Ho Chunk language.

But as important as language retention might have been to these Milwaukeeans, many families succumbed to the acculturation process, where fluency in the languages of past homelands was not valued.

*Mexican 115*: We were told that speaking Spanish should be an embarrassment. The schools didn't want it, the neighborhood didn't, and eventually our parents didn't.

*Italian 110*: So when my brother was old enough to go to school, he went to [Name] School. The teacher sent him home because he couldn't understand English, because all he heard all his life was the Italians talking. When my brother came home, my father was so hurt, because his main thing was to be an American, a good American. So from then on he says, "No more Italian in the house, we speak English." So that's why I never really learned the Italian language, because my folks never talked to us in Italian anymore.

Through the acculturation process, many participants in the study lost the languages.

*Jewish 112*: Well, aside from English, many of the older people spoke Yiddish back then. [In] my own community today, actually speaking Yiddish is rare. Some of us, the older, remember how to understand it. There are very few Yiddish speakers around now, but there were quite a few in the 1950s.

*American Indian Oneida 133*: Our challenge is language. . . . Only thirty-five of about fifteen thousand Oneida members here can speak it fluently. Language should go on to children.

Despite the pressures to abandon languages of past homelands, many local ethnic groups and their members struggled to preserve them. This does not mean that the languages remained unchanged.

*Norwegian 150*: To keep my native language going, I like to write to my friend and keep connection with my cousin's wife in Norway who has been very good about writing to me throughout all my years I have lived here. And also I have this friend that I took this trip with and stayed with her and she writes long letters and also very informative about what goes on in Norway and likewise I will tell her what goes on here.

*Polish 135*: The different blends in the city changed the language. Polish changed to reflect "Mitchell St. Polish"—English words with Polish ends. On Mitchell Street there were so many Jewish vendors. They had Yiddish words, and Poles doing business with them would pick up those words too. When my dad went back to Poland, people didn't understand him.

*Taiwanese 131*: Taiwanese language is originally from Chinese, but there are differences. Some people now speak the local language, and it's different from Mandarin. So we want to pass that to the second generation, especially if they are born in the States and look at themselves as American, not Taiwanese.

*German Russian 198*: We were in Russia before we came to the United States, but my great grandparents [in Russia], my grandparents, my parents, and me and my siblings kept the German language. But you know, it really must have changed. When we took a trip to Germany in 1993, it was hard to understand them and harder for them to understand us. I guess it was the way we had travelled all over and picked up little differences.

*Hmong 142*: We speak it at home. If you teach a kid English first and Hmong second they will get a huge accent and you can't understand them. If you teach them Hmong first and then English, then it works out.

*Palestinian 122*: I think our community has only taught the children Arabic. There was an understanding that as soon as they started going to school, they were going to learn English. Children pick up languages quickly. My parents brought schoolbooks from overseas. We studied Arabic growing up so we could read, write, and speak. I think Arabs have always been pretty proud to be Arab. There was never a fear of that. A lot of the people now can't read or write, but still speak it. I think there's efforts overall to maintain that, though. The kids who grew up here, some still have Arabic as their primary language.

In some cases clubs developed when enough Milwaukeeans wanted to work on language retention. See field notes below.

*Field Notes: January, 2008*
Every first Tuesday of the month a group gathered at the German [café] in Milwaukee. "Bertha" attended it as often as possible to meet other Germans or

German-speaking people. The group, usually about ten to twelve in number, represented all ages and all levels of German language proficiency. Included were native speakers, those who grew up bilingually in the United States, some who had stayed abroad in German-speaking countries, and also beginners who wanted to exercise their language skills. The gathering was organized to retain the language, practice one's skills, and also to meet people that shared something in common. The locations had German décor, sometimes played German music, and also offered German menu choices. Bertha said she was delighted to learn that others in Milwaukee had at least heard of the small town in Germany where she and her ancestors hailed.

# Relearning the Language

Since the multiculturalism movement took hold after the civil rights marches of the 1960s (Glazer, 1997), groups have experienced less pressure to speak only English. Many study participants talked about an emerging new pride in learning the languages of their former homelands.

> *African American 166*: Now we are seeing a growing interest in African languages—especially when someone has a clue about their origins through DNA or something. But there were languages built in North America by Africans. This would be Creole languages that were a combination of African languages—a kind of pidgin—and the languages of the colonists, the English, French, and I think the Dutch, probably more.

> *Chilean 155*: I sometimes wondered about Latinos who don't speak Spanish, and asked if they are Latinos. But I remember there are many different cultures that grow up in different ways. I think that a lot of Latinos are ashamed if they don't speak Spanish.

With growing interest in ethnic *everything*, many Milwaukee groups worked to revitalize the languages of the past. Ethnic organizations often offer classes. The number of language immersion, ethnic-specific, and bilingual schools in greater Milwaukee kept growing. Today it is not unusual to find discrete families and individuals also making the effort to relearn the language.

> *Chinese 171*: I speak the Cantonese dialect, but what they emphasize now is the Mandarin which is the national Chinese language. My children have taken classes through the church and in college a class or two.

> *North American Indian Ojibwe 100*: The only reason we still have an Ojibwe language today in Wisconsin is because the Canadian Ojibwe kept it up. Now a few of us are trying to relearn it.

> *German 121*: Well, for me, right now, I'm really in a romantic phase. I really like the German language. So I put a lot of time and energy trying to sharpen

my German language skills. That's personal. German was not spoken in my home. My family came over so long ago that not even my grandfather spoke German.

*Irish 184*: I learned Gaelic because my Irish ancestors originally spoke it. Not many Irish immigrants spoke Gaelic, but mine did. It was important to me to learn it.

## The Following Chapter

One of the most important reasons that the Milwaukee ethnics retained or re-learned the language of former homelands was to maintain ties to these regions. Chapter 5 describes the ways that these ties were kept.

# Chapter Five
# Ethnic Practices: Ties to Past Homelands

Immigrants anywhere have mixed motivations for settling in new lands. At times it is to escape economic hardship, political persecution, or social unrest. Sometimes the goal is simply seeking new opportunities and experiences. And at other times the immigrants settle in new areas with the intent to help those back home or return with more assets (e.g., Watson, 1974).

Regardless of the original motivations, many immigrant families continued to hold the homeland as their central frame of reference for standards of success, values, desired occupations, and forms of social organization. Many participants in the Milwaukee study maintained contact with families and friends back home. While ties weakened somewhat with each generation in the new land, they didn't disappear. An exception to this was the dilemma that African Americans faced.

## African Americans and Past Homelands

During the civil rights movements in the 1960s, some ethnic scholars began to advise blacks to develop their own history, which included roots in Africa (Hannerz, 1969; Karenga, 1968). But this was problematic. Although DNA research has made great strides in helping some African Americans identify their ancestral areas, few in the Milwaukee study had taken advantage of this new resource at the time they were interviewed. Participants discussed their frustrations trying to conceptualize their roots in Africa.

> *African American 126*: I know some blacks that have gone to Africa. But it's hard. You don't really know where you came from. You visit here. Was this my ancestor's home? Was this my ancestors' tribe? You come away with more questions than answers. I know people that have come back mad. They say, "Other people go to their home countries and search for their roots. We have nothing to search for."

*African American 129*: For most people, they say they like to know about their ancestors and where they came from and all. For us, we don't know. Our history was stripped from us. When I did genealogy in Kentucky where my great grandparents lived, I found I had an Irish ancestor. So it's silly, or maybe not, but I've taken more of an interest in Irish things lately. But I really want to know about my African roots. I hope that the new DNA rage changes that somehow. Maybe then we will have a better idea of who we are. Maybe then I can decide whether to send my daughter to learn dance at [African dance studio] or the [Irish dance studio]. [Laughter] I'm teasing. Or maybe not.

*African American 191*: Africans brought a culture with them and mixed it with American. It's not totally American but a blend. You can see [it] in syntax of black speech. But we still value unity. Rap music is a derivative of oral culture, when we were deprived of reading and writing. . . . Maybe everyone is a blend in some way. But usually other people at least know who they came from, where they came from. And for us, it's a mystery.

Most other study participants were able to maintain some ties to their past homelands. They helped relatives back home, traveled, or supported policies and humanitarian efforts that aided the former homelands.

# Helping Relatives

According to worldbank.com ("Migration & Remittances," 2013), approximately 3 percent of the world's population lives outside their countries of birth. Remittances, or the money sent back home, are three times the size of official development assistance, and the figures to developing nations in 2011 were estimated to be $372 billion. Among those in the Milwaukee sample living in the Diaspora, it was quite common for first-generation immigrants to send a portion of their earnings to relatives in former homelands. Some sent money back home after more than one generation.

*Mexican 193*: Oh we all sent money back to our relatives in Mexico when we first arrived. Some still send money twenty and thirty years later. . . . I have these music gigs. When I do them, all the money goes to my relatives in Mexico.

*Indian 142*: I used to send money home. . . . A lot of people do. Mostly, like when you get permanent, you care more. They put it in their own account so they can buy property.

*Slovak 140*: I know my ancestors sent money back home. I found these thank you letters that I had transcribed.

## Traveling to Past Homelands

Visiting past homelands was common among the Milwaukee informants. For some it meant reconnecting with relatives. For others it was a spiritual pilgrimage. And for still others it was an opportunity to learn more about the places where their ancestors once lived and about the past, generally.

> *North American Indian Menomonie 182*: It's important for many Indian people as well as myself to keep the ties to the rez. People might work here in Milwaukee and maintain a household, yet go home to the rez in summers. It's having a home in two places.

> *Palestinian 112*: They [thirty-seven grandchildren] have all been back to Palestine.

> *Jewish 124*: Many, many Jews have been to Israel. You rarely see an Orthodox family that has not been there.

> *German 143*: I teach the advanced German classes to adults. . . . In fact, in one class, there are five lawyers and two judges and they all know German. They are more or less fluent. Of course they make mistakes and they like to keep up with the German when they go to Germany and so on. I don't think anyone really needs it here [in the United States].

> *Chinese 171*: I think traveling is a major thing for many families. They travel back to see grandparents. Something that might be in my future is a trip back to China, to see the old country and see where you're from, and show the children where that part of their culture is from. I think that's always been a trek that families have taken when their children are older.

> *English 112*: I developed an interest in history by doing genealogy into my British ancestors. By the time I got to visit England and Scotland (oh, and Wales too), I knew the history of these areas and wanted to learn more. I got enthralled with Cornish history even though I don't think my ancestors came from there.

> *Norwegian 150*: Most Norwegians are very connected with their homeland still. So in other words, their old culture values still are staying with them, whoever they are. I know many Norwegians who have lived there many years. When they retire here and they can see how well Norway has developed, and then they retire by going back home. They retire to Norway.

## Supporting Efforts to Help Past Homelands

For some, ties to the old countries meant taking pride in homeland achievements. For others it meant supporting favorable policies and humanitarian efforts for the past homelands.

> *Taiwanese 111*: We were talking about fundraising for relief to the earthquakes in China. We did a big fundraiser before. We should send out something to help with that effort. We're going to be doing [name] teleconferencing house party. That's going to be on campus, so we'll be getting some Asian students there. The teleconference includes someone from the White House. They'll have a congressional representative from California, talking on his perspectives on the state of Asians today. Grassroots people will talk. Then we'll discuss what some of the issues are that we want addressed.

> *Italian 132*: When they had the earthquake in Italy and right away we were sending emails out and raising money for that. I think we try to keep a connection with Italy itself.

> *Polish 145*: International events have impacted the Polish community here. WWII was a turning point. There was the election of the Pope and the Solidarity movement in Poland, and that gave a big boost to our community. The [*Leonardo da Vinci and the*] *Art of Poland* art exhibit here was big. People can say, "We really are important." The Polish here have had an inferiority complex. It's important to have the outside world notice, like with Walensa and [the] Nobel Peace Prize.

## The Following Chapter

Chapter 6 discusses the relationships between past homelands and the religions of Milwaukee informants. In the United States, freedom of religion is guaranteed in the Bill of Rights (which failed early on to extend to African slaves and North American Indians), but this was not true in most former homelands of US immigrants. There, religions were often imposed on the citizenry by conquering forces, royal families, and legislation to institutionalize one religion. In most cases these religions were those that immigrants and their descendants continued to practice in America.

# Chapter Six
# Ethnic Practices: Religion

Gans (1979) used the term *sacred cultures* to describe ethnic groups with strong solidarity with particular religions, such as Poles, Irish, Arabs, Latinos, Greeks, Jews, Serbs, Lithuanians, and Armenians. According to Geertz (1963), social scientists should consider treating religion as a *cultural* system because it serves as a source of conceptions about the world, the self, and the relation between the two. Thus when most members of an ethnic group shared the same religion, the bonds of ethnicity strengthened significantly. Ethnic faith communities were more than just centers for ideology. In most cases, the church, synagogue, mosque, temple, and spiritual meeting hall served as a community center for immigrant groups. Baptist, Methodist, and (in Milwaukee) Catholic churches also helped African Americans by playing strong roles in advancing causes in the civil rights movements of the 1960s (Corbett, 1997).

The identification of religion with ethnicity has benefits, but it can also present a dilemma for some. While most immigrants travel with the same faith they acquired in some former homeland, they might encounter pressures during migration to change religions or drop them entirely in favor of a more secular life.

## Ethnicity and the Seculars

When a religion is identified too closely with an ethnic group, it can have confounding results. The Jews are one example. Is a person practicing the Jewish religion but having no ethnic Jews as ancestors considered a Jew? How does a person with Jewish ethnic ancestry, but does not practice the Jewish religion, have Jewish *culture* (Epstein, 1978)? Data suggest that only 57 percent of American Jews have synagogue affiliations (American Jewish Committee, 2005), a figure that may be lower today. To many participants in the Milwaukee study, Jewish culture had become overly identified with orthodoxy, a concern expressed by less conservative Jews elsewhere in the United States (Worth-heimer, 1993). This was particularly problematic at the time the Milwaukee interviews were conducted, as orthodoxy had been on the rise in Milwaukee County. An Orthodox individual described the growth.

*Jewish 101*: There were two specific movements that happened in Judaism which happened since the late 1960s. What you had in the 1960s in Milwaukee was a very strong periphery and a very weak core. You had a lot of Jews with an erosion of religiosity. One of the things that happened is that Jews gained greater freedom in America, which turned out to be the curse of intermarriage and assimilation which occurred at that time. We were insulated from the factors of anti-Semitism. Today you have a weak periphery and that core is very strong. The core is a dramatic growth of orthodoxy.

However, with Jewish holidays, history, and rites of passage intensely infused with religion, some secular Jews questioned their identity.

*Jewish 124*: Maybe we secular Jews need to decide exactly what *our* culture is. If we are not religious, in what ways are we Jews? What are our common denominators?

*Jewish 181*: Take the religion completely out of the equation and we're left with just the negative stereotypes—Jews as tradesmen, wanderers, outsiders, whatever.

*Jewish 184*: Most of the Orthodox keep their own version of Jewish culture by isolating themselves from others. The secular [Jews] struggle with this. If we are not particularly spiritual, where do we have culture?

Among some Russian Jews, another issue emerged. Those who emigrated from the former Soviet Union had been denied the opportunity to practice Judaism. Lacking the religion, often for generations, some preferred the ethnic designation of Russian.

*Russian 125*: Some of the Russian speaking here in Milwaukee are practicing [the] Jewish religion. They attend synagogue. I know Lithuanians have their own church and Ukrainians also have their own church. I don't believe in God so I believe in judicial democracy. . . . But remember, back in the USSR in order to get a college degree—in order to graduate from college—you have to take two courses in [the] history of communism and the theory of agnostic thought.

*Russian 127*: I am not a Jew. I was a Jew in the USSR because my grandparents were Jews. Here I say I am a Russian speaking person—a Russian. I don't practice the Jewish religion.

However, for most study participants from other groups, religion and ethnicity could be decoupled without the risk of ambiguous identities. In some cases, individuals retreated from the religion of their past homeland and became secular; at other times they changed religious practices; in other cases their homeland sects were too diverse to be considered ethnic religions. But in any case, the study participants still identified with their ethnic groups.

*German 140*: Most of the Germans I happen to know well aren't very religious. My *Oma* [grandmother] is Catholic, and her husband, a Serb, converted to Catholicism from the Serbian Orthodox Church when they married in the forties. They were more frequent in their church attendance when they still lived in Germany up to 1955. After they moved to the US, I don't recall hearing about an active church presence. That being said, my *Oma* still self-identifies as a Catholic and would probably describe religion as an important part of her life. My mom and her sister were raised Catholic, but both left the church for the most part when they reached their teens. The Germans I know well enjoy going to church for the main masses at Christmas and Easter, but not much else.

*Hmong 132*: We were animists. Christianity was introduced in the 1950s in Laos—late 1950s. It's fairly new to us. About 65 percent here are Christian and 35 percent practice a belief in ancestor worship. They believe that when ancestors die they become good spirits and come back to help others. People offer to ancestors, offer incense, a small meal to ask good spirits to share meal with them. [They] burn special paper from way back in Chinese history, will transfer this into money to good spirit to have a means of purchasing things. [It's] very popular in this group. Hmong culture has different ways of marriage ceremonies and funerals. Even though some are Christian, they practice cultural parts of celebrations.

*French 120*: I know some who go to church. I know some who are absolute atheists. Basically, the French people don't think much of the Church. Most of the French people I know, for them, church is not a consideration. But there are a lot, and also in this Francophone community that I mentioned, a lot of our Francophone Africans are very religious people. . . . I go to a church sometimes with a cousin of my husband's. Everyone who comes to me speaks French. It's a kind of gathering place for the Francophone community. They say that the French here go to church for baptism, marriage, and death—and nothing in between.

*German 170*: There are the strongest elements of the retention of the German culture to be found in German Catholicism and German Lutheran religions. The North Germans who were Calvinists have more or less become assimilated in the United Church of Christ. . . . Then there was the German freethinking society of which there are a few remnants left in Milwaukee.

However, the vast majority of study participants in Milwaukee County claimed that religious practices helped them retain their ethnicity. The ethnic-enhancing practices took place both in private through symbols and in public through faith communities.

## Private Consolidation of Religion and Ethnicity

Study participants discussed the religious practices they observed with their family or alone. In most cases these practices were those they carried over from their past homelands.

> *Italian 135:* But today, if you look at it and try and find a trend, and try to understand the power of the relationship of religion to Italian culture, it's always been at the center of Italian culture. From the naming of children after Italian saints to very traditional events, holidays, methods by which you conduct your life.

> *Palestinian 159:* I have a mix of religious family and friends. And I also have secular Arab friends too. It's a personal decision for Arabs living in America or in Palestine. But even those who don't pray five times per day as required, we all mostly fast during the holy month of Ramadan.

> *Greek 172:* In their homes we have special areas with shelves where they have their family altar with icons, like of Jesus, the Virgin Mary, and patron saints of members of the family. We light it with lights and keep the holy water from the church on special occasions. This is another place for the family to pray. It is a family-based worship. And we follow certain traditions like baking a special bread to be used in divine liturgies. We make boiled wheat with some sweet stuff in it like raisins. If we have someone buried here in Milwaukee, we take some of that wheat and throw it on the grave.

> *North American Indian Oneida 160:* It's most important practice is staying connected with my creator, and the connection to mother earth. I see that every day we're here is a gift. I am happy every day I get up. I acknowledge that each morning to our grandmothers and our creator. We smudge, and burn cedar and sage grass. . . . We want our creator to see this. We appreciate the medicines they give us.

> *Slovak 141:* We do not have Slovak services at our Lutheran church anymore, but I do make the *oplatky* or Christmas wafers for the Slovaks that still attend there. They are eaten on Christmas Eve with honey before we eat our meal.

## Public Consolidation of Religion and Ethnicity

However, most practices that consolidated religion and ethnicity occurred in public, mostly in faith communities. In some cases, events focused on ethnically-specific ways to celebrate religious holidays, such as the example below from field notes.

*Field Notes: April, 2012*
In late afternoon, the day before Easter, a group of several hundred mainly Polish worshippers began entering the [Catholic church] on Milwaukee's south side to assemble in a lower level sanctuary. Nearly everyone was carrying a large basket, lined with white linens, and covered with a cloth. In the baskets were food and drink for their Easter breakfast and treats for the children's Easter baskets. As the services ensued, the priest began his annual blessing of the Easter baskets, systematically blessing each food and drink item by category, and walking down the aisle sprinkling holy water from a wand in the direction of the baskets.

I was told that the custom of blessing the baskets, called *swieconka* in Polish, is one of the most enduring customs brought over from Poland, and goes back to medieval times in Europe.

Informants from the Milwaukee study also discussed ethnically specific ways they celebrated religious holidays.

*Filipino 131*: During Holy Week there are a number of special services that the [name of organization] offers in our language. We do have a Filipino center on [name of street]. That is where we host the most events. In the Filipino tradition, on the nine days before Christmas we go to mass every single day. It's called night mass or *Simbang Gabi*. That's the one I wouldn't miss. It's a big deal back home. The events are centered around religion. We have some Muslims, Protestants, but mostly Catholics.

*Polish 151*: The Catholic Church is involved in all parts of our lives. It's life centered on the parish. We had sixteen to eighteen Polish parishes then in the city, and still have several. Food traditions are big. Mom was [a] great cook. We'd have kielbasa at holidays. We'd have manger straw and have some shafts of straw under the tablecloth, and an empty place. The idea was open hospitality for people. And there was the Feast of Corpus Christi. We'd have an outdoor altar and processions from altar to altar. And there was Fat Tuesday—the Tuesday before Ash Wednesday—the day where all families baked *paczki*, jelly-filled donuts where we'd use up all the lard and flour and sugar and so on.

*Nepali 198*: Last couple of *Dashains* [Hindu religious festival], I have had my parents here with us, so we did all the rituals and regular *pujas* [offerings] during the entire period of Dashain. . . . My family then visits my in-laws elsewhere in the US. So, at family scale, it is much like what we used to have back in Nepal.

*Puerto Rican 154*: For Puerto Ricans here, Holy Week, which is between Palm Sunday and Easter [is important]. Palm Sunday is the day Christ enters Jerusalem, and he has the last supper and is crucified. Forty days before resurrection, or Lent, there are traditions that are kept. We don't dance, and eat only certain things. People say if you dance during that week your legs will become thin, and so on.

The day before the feast of Saint John, people in Puerto Rico go to the beach and take a dip at midnight. It goes back to the Spanish traditions of Saint John the Baptist—it's like you are getting baptized. But it really is a combination with the African, because it's not totally a Christian tradition. It's taking St. John the Baptist, but at the same time you're throwing yourself in the water seven times for good luck, which is more of the African tradition.

*Lithuanian 199*: My favorite and most important cultural practice is Christmas Eve. I actually thought every Catholic country practiced the same Christmas, only when I came to the United States did I realize this wasn't true. Christmas Eve, every Lithuanian cleans their house in and out, have to give "all the debts away"—pay your debts. At the end of the day you shower and put on clean clothes, and put down a white tablecloth for family dinner, and extra plates are put out for family who is no longer with us, before the meal there is prayer. We get communion and eat bread with each other, and wish the best and give kisses to each other around the table. We all say "Happy Christmas" to each other. Then, some food is left on the table for the ones who have passed away. Because, they say that the souls come at midnight or after midnight to visit and eat the food. Grandma used to say "that's the only night animals speak, but if you hear them, you will die."

In other cases, the faith communities also functioned as gathering places for families of the same ethnic background—the emphasis being on the social.

*Indian 121*: We do have a temple. I can see how church is important for Christians, right? Temple is important for Hindus. There's a temple in [town outside of Milwaukee]. There are loads of Indians staying there and [another nearby town], so it's convenient for them to just come. We used to go mostly weekends, every weekend, for no reason. "Let's just go, and if they need help we will go help, if they need volunteers. If they are doing some functions there we can just go and help make their function better." So it's not just religious necessarily—maybe social. There are loads of religions in India, but once you are out of India, everything is the same. Here I celebrate all Indian festivals, not just the ones from my state. In India each state is very different. Each one has its own language and it will be totally different. You can't understand a word. It's like if I went to Texas and I couldn't understand one word. Yes, food, religion, gods are different. Every state will have their [sic] own kind of stuff. What I realized once I was out of India is I am just Indian. I will celebrate everything.

*Puerto Rican 104*: Most of our cultural practices come through the church. It is the primary way. I think most social organizations stem from there in terms of who knows who, and who belongs to which clique. The church is the meeting place for a lot of families and their extended families.

*Italian 114*: Italians will go to Sunday mass and everything. They don't treat it just as a Sunday mass. It's more as a gathering place to meet people afterwards, so it's part religious, part social. I've also been asked to help with the church festival at [name of church], to resurrect it. There's also a society called the [name] club that I am involved with.

*Jewish 139*: We have over one hundred Jewish families that came together in this neighborhood, that are members of [name of synagogue]. A lot are young with lots of kids. It's a conglomerate of people from all over the country.

*African American 143*: We are evangelicals, Jehovah's Witnesses, Pentecostals, Catholic, Muslims, Methodists, Baptists—you name it. When we are in the church, we are *really* in the church. We aren't like Caucasians where we go to church for form, because it looks good. If we feel that way, we leave the church. When we are in it, we are really in it. Our services last until they are done. We don't keep set times. We get into it and the preacher can preach as long as it suits him or the choir can sing as long as they want.

*Mexican 184*: There is a huge difference between black, Anglo, and Latino celebrations. We are very strong with the church. We live around the church. Much of the strength of our community comes from faith and practicing our religion. I live at the church; it is my home. We go more than five times a week.

In still other cases, the faith communities initiated events that were secular in nature.

*Italian 147*: Religious groups were primarily responsible for providing assistance to new immigrants with socializing, general skill building, learning the English language, and becoming citizens. Most of the festivals and societies that were present in the past, and may have carried on until today, are religious-based.

*Greek 123*: Both churches have Greek festivals. [Name of church] has a huge Greek fest. They had to move it to the state fair grounds because the area was getting bad and it got rowdy. They had to shut down the midway. [Another church] has its fair. One year they transported it to a park in [Milwaukee suburb] but that wasn't economically feasible. There was [name of organization] and some women's groups. There's one group of people that came from the same areas where my folks were born and they meet periodically. Both churches have young children do Greek dances and have Greek food.

While no study participants suggested that the faith communities lacked attention to their sacred duties, some implied that the ethnic spotlight was sometimes more important to parishioners than religion.

*Greek 180*: Well, I think they love the Orthodox Church, but I don't know how serious many are. One archbishop told me this: "Some only go on Easter and Good Friday. Sometimes we worship the Greek language rather than God." . . . People love the Greek Orthodox religion though. We have the right doctrine from the apostles, but we aren't that serious about it.

*Serbian 155*: It is a *Serbian* church. You listen to what I said. I didn't say it was a *church*. We think that a church tends to the will of God. But if you have an ethnic church, well . . . [informant raises arms].

## The Following Chapter

Using national survey data in the late twentieth century, Andrew Greeley (1974) found that ethnicity was more likely to influence behavior than religion, but religion clearly played an important role for many in retaining ethnic ways. Equally important is food, the subject of chapter 7. Many of the foods still prepared and consumed by Milwaukee informants had long traditions in religious holidays. Cultural practices are always integrated, and food is especially so. Food also plays an interesting role in ethnic memory, as will be discussed in the chapter.

# Chapter Seven
# Ethnic Practices: Food

According to Mintz and Du Bois (2002), there has been a staggering increase in the literature on the anthropology of food since the early 1980s. The literature focuses on a wide range of topics. Foods consumed express a variety of messages about the individual and the culture, including statements about identity, methods in which food traditions are passed down, seasonality of food, use of food in rewards and punishments, foods and social status, contexts in which foods are being consumed, and ways that foods ease immigrant integration into the American mainstream (Farb and Armelagos, 1980; Humphrey and Humphrey, 1991; Toussaint-Samat, 2009). Milwaukee informants discussed personal meanings of ethnic food, and ways that foods led to greater sociality and increased acceptance of their groups in the United States.

## Personal Meaning of Ethnic Foods

To many participants in the Milwaukee study, preferences for the food of their ethnic groups were either a result of how their tastes developed in earlier years or statements about ethnic pride.

*Japanese 157*: Even though we can handle most of the Western foods, we get cravings every now and then. A lot of us go to this Japanese grocery store called [name of store], owned by Chinese, in the Chicago area. Many of us take a trip once in a while and buy Japanese ingredients that are not available in *normal* American stores.

*Russian 105*: I would say just keeping the Russian mentality is a major part of how I live. The generosity and hospitality are major aspects—and of course, the food. I would not be the same without my mother's Russian cooking. It's how I was raised.

*Chinese 171*: Growing up we all wanted to just fit in. We were just learning and helping our parents fit in at the same time. None of those concerns were really

prevalent. We did things a little differently than everyone else. It was to varying degrees. I didn't face too much discrimination so it was pretty comfortable.
My mom was very up to date with all the newest American ways and styles so
we had no problem that way, but I knew we did things differently. Not everyone ate with a rice bowl or chopsticks and the foods that we ate were different.
I didn't really feel anything different. However in my twenties I just wanted a
connection with others that were similar. Then trying to think how I would
raise my children, and how I was going to incorporate [Chinese eating styles].

*Norwegian 198*: I guess the most important [ethnic practice] is the passing on
of some of the special things and I guess what I brought from my own parents
or the foods and the making of the foods. . . . And I would think the passing on
of the recipes of the foods.

*Hmong 135*: We still eat the foods from old country—rice, vegetables. You see
Hmong gardening a lot—home-grown vegetables. I do my own gardening.

But to some study participants, consuming ethnic foods had an almost
transcendent meaning. Sutton (2001) asks that scholars simultaneously consider
food and memory in understanding cultural processes. He argues that the taste and
smell of food, having a greater association with episodic and symbolic memory
than semantic and linguistic memory, help to explain how they encode (and
subsequently release) memories of past contexts.

*Jewish 179*: My family has not been spiritual since my grandmother was alive.
But for some reason or other we still want the foods at the various times of
year. We sometimes do the Seder even though we aren't sure that we're committed to the religious parts. My kids loved getting the matzo at that time of
year. We just loved it. We always had the potato pancakes at Hanukkah and
would eat apples and honey at the Rosh Hashanah. It's funny. We never think
about special foods at any other time of the year. It's like you have a craving
for that food then and something about tasting it connects you to your childhood and maybe a distant past. It's very fulfilling.

*German 182*: My family has not cooked German for, oh, several decades. Yet
every so often we get the desire for German food and find our way to one of the
German restaurants around town. I'm not sure why it's so satisfying. It's more
than a craving for a food that you like. The entire taste brings you back—back
to a time of Sunday dinners. Or maybe it's just the need to connect to something larger than myself.

*Slovenian 192*: Eating strudel or potica, or just grilled chicken, with all of the
associated tastes, smells, textures, and maybe the process of preparing them,
brings alive experiences we had with our parents or grandparents. Culture isn't
just a memory of another time; it's tangible, shared experiences.

In some ways, the link between food and memory may also connect to the sociality of food.

# Sociality of Ethnic Foods

Holtzman (2006, p. 373) asks this question: "What makes food such a powerful and diffuse locus of memory?" Citing literature on how American ethnic identities are maintained and performed through food, he agrees with many that the sensuality of eating transmits mnemonic cues through tastes and smells, but suggests that there is something more significant to the link. He states that one potential might be the extent to which food traverses the public and the intimate realms.

> Although eating always has a deeply private component, unlike our other most private activities food is integrally constituted through its open sharing, whether in rituals, feasts, reciprocal exchange, or contexts in which it is bought and sold. One might consider then the significance of this rather unique movement between the most intimate and the most public in fostering food's symbolic power, in general, and in food's relation to memory, in particular. (p. 373)

The sociality of food, and its advance from the intimate to the communal, is a topic that the Milwaukee participants discussed in depth. Many talked about small ethnic dinner parties (often potlucks) or holiday family meals that had some connection to tradition, but tended to be informal and variable in context (Sherman, 1991). These intimate gatherings were ways for a few members of ethnic groups to gather to share food and stories about past homelands, sacred or historical events, and ethnic practices.

*Russian 151*: Well, I guess food is a big part of it, so we have dinner parties. Those times we'll often discuss books and music. Sometimes we'll watch movies and talk about them. I'm not really sure how different it is from other places. I would say, I lived in Chicago for a period of time and it was kind of similar there.

*African Congo Congolese 101*: We go to church and eat together Congo food at a potluck. We talk about information about the Congo and how to help each other. We talk about personal issues and what is going on back home. We socialize about everything, we all have problems and this is how to deal with them.

*African American 122*: People offer people food when they go to their homes—greens, sweet potatoes, macaroni and cheese, corn bread. I eat these when I'm alone, but it's more meaningful when we get together. Then we can talk about old times or things that interest black people.

*Italian 130*: Every function centers around a huge Italian dinner. Everything that you do has to be somehow linked to an Italian dinner or centered around food. They are very excited about their food. They are very excited about their gardens and the tomatoes that they grow to make their food. So food is just a huge, huge part of their culture.

*Chilean 182*: That's how you create a community—a lot of love and affection, physical like hugging, and making sure to take care of you with food. There is always food.

*Palestinian 152*: But the food thing—even in college. I remember when my friends would come over. You know I'd go home and change to leave again. I started making my friends wait in the car, because my mom was preparing a meal for them. You go to someone's house and you end up having to eat, drink, and sit down.

Some study participants described ways that the more intimate meals moved into larger feasts. Others discussed feasts organized around ethnic holidays or special events.

*North American Indian Potawatomi 162*: We see a lot of feasting coming back now in the city. There used to be intimate feasts but now we do a lot bigger ones and the community can come out. We put our differences aside to do this. We agree to disagree. A feast, not a potluck. A general feast can be like after a graduation ceremony or it's a traditional feast where all people bring something but where those hosting the feast bring the most. At funerals everyone brings the food but the family is mostly responsible. The potluck is where, if you have it, you bring it. A feast is more organized. Feasts are after a ceremony whereas the potluck is more informal. Potlucks are just a getting-together and eating, but even if we are in urban areas we are mindful of our food and the oldest person or spiritual person may bless our food.

*African American 188*: Blacks all over have picnics and things where we bring the chicken and the greens and salads and a lot [of] sweet potato pies. They're more like a potluck. My grandmother talked about the large teas that they used to have in the Bronzeville days. These would be feasts to honor people in the black community or raise funds.

*Indian 121*: We try to stick with our Indian food, because as you are aware, Indian food preparation is a little bit difficult and takes too much time. We like to do lots of get-togethers, especially for festivals. We like to hold the get-together on the day where the festival is. India will have the holy day on the festival, even if it's maybe a Tuesday. We like to dress up in our Indian outfits, because that's the only time we can wear them here. We'll have foods and we'll have everything that's kind of Indian.

# Food and Integration into the American Mainstream

Kalcik (1984) describes how the continued consumption of ethnic foods helps ease the immigrant's shock of living in a new country. But in order to maintain the diet, the ethnic group must open its own restaurants and food stores. Participants in the Milwaukee study described how these new ventures actually led to economic opportunities for groups.

> *Greek 123*: You'll find a lot of family restaurants that are Greek-owned in Milwaukee. Probably even half that we think of as just "family restaurants" are actually Greek-owned and offer a variety of Greek dishes.

> *Italian 113*: You see the restaurants, and the bakeries—all types of stuff—sprinkled throughout the city. It's really quite a few of them, if you think about it. It's ridiculous—the number—when you really think about it. It's probably one third of all restaurants are some Italian named restaurant that serves pizza right? I mean think about it, it's probably a good percentage of them.

> *Arab 122*: If we start with cuisine, especially on the East Side, there's a big influence—Middle Eastern food is very well liked, and there are a number of restaurants over there.

The food establishments often led to greater acceptance of the ethnic group in the United States and connected them to members of other ethnic groups.

> *Mexican 114*: We try to share our culture so that someday (and it is already beginning), as evidenced by the Spanish language incorporated into English and the commonplace of Mexican food in the American diet, we can gain acceptance.

> *Serbian 188*: I don't know if many in Milwaukee would even know there are Serbs here, except that there are Serbian restaurants. Our restaurants also attract patrons whose ancestors came from the Mediterranean and other Eastern European areas, as the foods are similar. We get connected to a lot of groups through the restaurants.

> *Russian 151*: And food is really a bonding experience, especially for such a diverse community like ours. You have a lot of ethnic restaurants, and food is one way that it is often introduced to us, in a way that's rather non-intrusive.

> *Mexican 114*: Because right now, Mexican food is very popular. Everywhere you go there is Mexican food, even at McDonald's.

> *Italian 144*: A lot of different ethnic groups would spring businesses together, for example, the food businesses. The Italians had started on a small scale, [and] had peddling businesses, Sicilian fruit companies, and what not. And they

have kind of worked together, in Milwaukee's case, with Jewish wholesalers. [Names] were kind of the big players.

## The Following Chapter

Food is, to most people, one of many art forms. This chapter gave it special distinction because it permeates the heart of ethnic life. Chapter 8 will discuss additional art forms with ethnic significance in the Milwaukee study.

# Chapter Eight
# Ethnic Practices: Art Forms

Ethnic art forms are people's attempts to define themselves and their place in the world—both factors driven by social and historical circumstances (Schnell, 2003). The art form can be as complex as theatrical productions and basilicas or as down-to-earth as yard art and body tattoos (Evans-Cowley and Nasar, 2003). For the Milwaukee participants, the art fulfilled many needs, including self-expression, ethnic pride, sociality, entertainment, and the transmission of history and folklore.

*Milwaukee Ethnic News*, a bimonthly newsletter published by Urban Anthropology (http://www.urban-anthropology.org/EthnicNewsletter.html), posts upcoming events in the ethnic arts. Typically, the summer festivals of over twenty ethnic groups feature crafts, music, dancing, storytelling, culinary arts, and literature. These activities do not end at the first frost. During the winter months of 2012/2013, ethnic art events featured in *Milwaukee Ethnic News* included (but were not limited to) the following: (1) a play on the Fair Housing Marches of the 1960s that placed Milwaukee African Americans and Poles in conflict, (2) art forms created to memorialize the Sikhs who died in the Oak Creek temple shooting, (3) a public performance by a Creek nation poet, (4) a Welsh singing performance, (5) book signings by authors of Polish American books, (6) four films shown on Slovak and Czech culture, (7) a series of performances by Puerto Rican musicians, (8) an exhibition of Polish violin and piano music, (9) a play on French chanteuse Edith Piaf, (10) a dance and music recital of the Danube Cultural society held at a Croatian church, (11) culinary arts exhibitions by major Italian chefs, (12) a Christmas multi-ethnic dance fest, (13) an exhibit of Polish Christmas crafts, (14) an art show at a Mexican gallery, (15) a drumming and dance performance by Wisconsin Indians, (16) African and African American poetry readings, (17) ethnic dancing and art at a Muslim women's event, (18) the restoration of the Polish Kosciuszko statue, (19) a play about early Armenian immigrants to Milwaukee, and (20) blocks of Irish dancers and musicians at the St. Patrick's Day parade. In addition, the Milwaukee County Park system opened its Mitchell Park horticultural domes during the winter to Polish, German, and Turk artists and organizations. The three events, with dancing, crafts, paintings, culinary exhibits, and bands, drew nearly ten thousand admission-paying people to the park, helping to support a county department in need of funds.

The informants in the Milwaukee study discuss their own art forms in the following sections on visual and performance art.

# Visual Arts

The Milwaukeeans described a variety of ethnic visual art forms, including paintings, sculpture, photography, architecture, jewelry, textiles, ceramics, furniture, drawing, and tattoos.

*Norwegian 176*: Well, mine [leisure time activity] would be rosemaling. . . . It's been thirty-six years. And that is my greatest pastime. . . . In Norway there are different types of rosemaling according to the different districts in Norway. So there's many different styles, but I would say five popular ones.

*North American Indian Oneida 122*: Beading really reached a high level with Wisconsin Indians. I would say mostly with the Oneida. I've seen people spend a year on one piece. Some people get together for beading circles where they bring potluck dishes and work on their beading. It's a great way to socialize while you work on your art. I've been to some where they play powwow music in the background.

*Polish 191*: We had a special art form we brought from Poland, called *wycinanki*. It was done by cutting out colored paper and layering the cutouts into forms. It's still taught to the new generations.

*Mexican 196*: There's Mexican tattoo parlors now and I have several of them [tattoos]—one on my arm and one on my back. I think it's a way to show I'm proud to be Mexican. But there's been a lot of problems in Milwaukee with graffiti people trying to be respected as artists, and that's not just Mexican graffiti.

*Mexican 190*: We have one of the most beautiful art galleries in the city. It's called [name], and art from all over the Latin world is exhibited there, including some local. My favorite time of the year for art is the *Dia de los Muertos*.

*German 160*: In Milwaukee the Germans were celebrated architects. So many of our great buildings go back to the days when Milwaukee was called the German Athens—City Hall, the Basilica, Turner Hall. [They were] all designed by German architects—Baroque, German Renaissance Revival.

*Hmong 155*: [My] wife does this, sews traditional clothing. I don't do anything. Wife tries to pass on to kids. Only time we wear traditional clothes is on New Year. In Laos [we] wore these more often. . . . And we started these story cloths back in the camps. Men would draw little figures that meant something from the old time and women would stitch them together to make story. Today some Hmong sell at markets. But most [are] made by machine now.

*African American 192*: Textile clubs were always big in the African American community. [We] brought them up from the South. Today there's still at least one quilting club that connects people to the old times. There was a really big one back about forty, fifty years ago—a kind of needlework club. I think it stopped maybe around 1990 or so, maybe later, but they did a lot of good work—gave the proceeds to help black kids get scholarships. Lots of other things.

# Performing Arts

The Milwaukee participants also described their involvement in a variety of ethnic performing arts, including opera, choirs, bands, theatre, dance, poetry readings, and storytelling.

*Italian 110*: Many years ago I used to belong to the [Name] Opera Chorus. Before it was the [Name] Opera, it was the [Name] Chorus and it was led by [name] who was my cousin and then during the war, instead of being Italian since Italians were fighting too, we changed it to the [Name] Opera. That's how it got its name, during World War Two. And my father joined it, and my husband joined it, and those were happy, happy years.

*Latvian 166*: Singing is to Latvians what baseball is to Americans. Everyone does it. It requires no equipment or expense and I have sung in Latvian for all of my life.

*German 111*: Even though [my parents] were born in the United States and I have never spoken German myself, I do sing some German songs. Often at your ski club programs we all get together and we sing *Bayern, Des Samma Mir* and some of the famous hall drinking songs.

*Welsh 103*: Hymn singing is an extremely important part of the culture. . . . The *Gymanfa Ganu* singing festival brings Welsh hymn singing to the general population.

*Taiwanese 131*: In Milwaukee, maybe because of the big city and the cultural focus, a lot of parents ask their kids to learn the traditional music of Taiwan. I was amazed at how the parents are focused on passing the cultural tradition to their children.

*African Nigerian Yoruba 101*: I would say poetry might be our most important ethnic practice here. I have gone to some poetry shows and you know and I've seen a lot of Africans and they are into poetry and stuff.

*Italian 138*: I have been in the Italian dance group of Milwaukee . . . I have been with them since I was eight and I'm forty now. I love folk dancing, love Italian folk dancing, love the music. I'm excited every Tuesday when I come here to dance. Every Tuesday, all I can think about is going to Italian dance class on Tuesday nights. And this has been going on what for thirty-two years now. I'm still as excited as I was when I was eight about it. I love it, I love it so much.

Many participants in the Milwaukee study emphasized a certain essence that made the ethnic art form unique.

*African American 178*: Jazz and blues are from memory and is still like this. With Europeans it's different—succinctly—they will play the same song twice exactly the same. This won't be the case with African Americans. It's how we see the world.

*Puerto Rican 134*: I play with various groups throughout the city, particularly my own, a Latin jazz group, and a *bomba* and *plena* group, which is strictly Afro-Puerto Rican music. And a little salsa, meringue, funk, whatever.

*North American Indian Ojibwe 162*: For a lot of American Indians there are coyote trickster stories that we tell. But most Indians use storytelling to make points—whether that's to stop drinking or honor your elders or respect the earth. Anything.

*Irish 155*: Irish stories can go on for days. We have this event close to Halloween, called *Samhain,* where we all go out to the woods, gather around a campfire, and listen to Irish stories, some of them very mystical.

*African American 132*: I've been in many black plays. I like the way that some of them bring in rap and rhyming to show our roots. Some talk about our history. One play was about the way blacks first lived when they came to Milwaukee. There's been a couple about the civil rights marches.

As with all cultural forms, the arts of the ethnic groups adapt to changes in the larger culture.

*German 101*: We take plays and actually kind of translate them now into the American language, a little bit—if that's possible—and present them. They're mostly a comedy type thing. Because of the variety shows that are being put on here in Milwaukee, they have to be visual, they have to be funny, they have to be—whatever. Nobody sits through a Ludwig Toma play anymore. It's just all too serious, you know.

## The Following Chapter

As diverse as art forms are among informants in the Milwaukee study, so are healing practices. Chapter 9 focuses on healthcare and healing, as described by the Milwaukee informants. These topics are very integrated with religion and food, as many ethnic beliefs about healing involve supernatural forces and edible plants.

# Chapter Nine
# Ethnic Practices: Healthcare and Healing

Since the late nineteenth century, anthropologists and other scholars have published works on healing, shamanism, and the cultural influences on medical beliefs. By the 1930s the cultural components of medical systems became a prominent dimension in American cultural anthropology (Rubel and Hass, 1990).

Definitions of health can vary across ethnic lines. According to Lewis (2001), ethnic groups have their own accepted ideas about (a) the nature of their bodies, (b) diet, (c) risk factors to health, (d) dangers of the environment, (e) child development, (f) health taboos, (g) theories about energy, and (h) harmony and balance. Among some ethnic groups, illness can be blamed on the malevolence of witches or sorcerers (Helman, 2001). Ferraro (1998, p. 303) points out that beliefs about the supernatural often affect ideas of health and healing.

> These supernatural explanations can take a number of different forms, including attributing illness to witches, evil spirits, the wrath of god, voodooism, dead ancestors, and bad magic. How these folk beliefs and explanations are dealt with by members of the Western, scientifically based medical community influences the effectiveness of the health systems they design for culturally distinct populations.

But folk beliefs about healthcare are not necessarily inaccurate nor are they dying out. Anderson (1997) summarizes traditional medical values of food in China over the centuries and maintains that some of these ideas were very close to what is known today scientifically, as in the heating and cooling properties of calories. Moreover, Trotter and Chavira (1997) studied *curanderismo,* a Mexican folk healing system, in south Texas and argue that the practices are not on the decrease but clearly increasing in some areas.

Participants in the Milwaukee study offered very diverse opinions about (and experiences with) Western healthcare and ethnic medical beliefs. It was not uncommon for one individual in a cultural group to claim use of folk healing alone, another of the same group to claim use of Western medicine alone, and another to claim use of both. Nor were individuals whose families emigrated from developing nations more likely to restrict their health practices to folk medicine than individuals whose families emigrated from other areas.

# Attitudes about Western Medicine

Some informants claimed they only used Western medicine for healthcare, whether this use was in the United States or in their former homelands.

*Scottish 151*: Well, if you are talking about the US—Scots living here—they are probably in the pretty much same mode as we all are in terms of health insurance, health care, you know, visits to the doctor that sort of thing. In Scotland itself the medical care is actually rather excellent. There are several very prominent medical schools in Scotland so you see a great number of good doctors being turned out from there.

*African Congo Congolese 122*: In Congo, the healthcare system is very modern. We go to the hospital and don't believe in witchcraft. We all go to standard hospitals. The Congo is a very civilized and modern country in Africa.

*Norwegian 156*: I don't know of anybody that I know of personally that if you have a healthcare problem you don't go to the doctor. You are just probably killing yourself. It's a thing that you can't just put it on the wayside. Your health is important.

*German 117*: Most have health care like anyone else in Milwaukee. They do go to the doctor when they need to and most have coverage.

*Cuban 161*: We [Cubans] are still one of the leading countries in regards to research and medicine. We are on the cutting edge of medicine and education, even at this point, because it is something we value very highly. Same with Cubans here—we value education and health care. We go to the doctor if we have health issues.

While most in the Milwaukee sample used Western medicine at least for some health concerns, others were critical of *American* healthcare. Some did not trust it, and sometimes as the result of past experiences. For example, African Americans had been subjected to the infamous Tuskegee syphilis experiment for forty years, beginning in 1932. Impoverished black men in Macon County, Alabama—399 with diagnosed syphilis and 201 without the disease—were recruited for a study where they were given free medical care, meals, and free burial insurance. Those with syphilis were never told they had the disease and were never treated for it. Many died and passed the disease on to partners and children. Locally, abuses of African Americans in the healthcare system and other US institutions were made public in America's Black Holocaust Museum on Milwaukee's north side (now an online museum).

*African American 139*: I think there's a little less trust of your American healthcare practices among blacks because they think about the times they were used in experiments. There's just not the trust. A lot of people from the South brought up their own roots and herbs and some of these are still used today.

*African American 144*: If you look at our history, you can understand why some brothers and sisters don't trust it.

Informants from other ethnic groups found the US healthcare system inaccessible or, at times, inferior to what they'd known in their former homeland.

*Russian 120*: The healthcare in the Soviet Union was possibly the best healthcare in the world considering the totality of circumstances. It wasn't so expensive as it is here and was affordable, as everybody was covered. So we are kind of accustomed to the healthcare and we are accustomed to medical professions since the medical profession was very popular in the former USSR.

*English 113*: We consider it very bad luck to have to live in a country that doesn't have it [easy access to healthcare].

*Mexican 115*: In Mexico, the government takes care of the healthcare. And so it's all pretty much taken care of there. Here, in America, many Mexicans don't have well-paying jobs with healthcare benefits. So they can't afford decent healthcare or good insurance a lot of times.

*African Tanzanian Kurian 141*: It can be expensive, very expensive, so even if they do have access to it, it's really not accessible and not everyone has the health insurance, but also some have their own cultural belief, and a lot of times it stays with them. Preventive care is not something that most people focus on. It's more on emergency case. If they really are suffering and they really can't take it, that's when most of them will go to the hospital.

*Russian 144*: They do not trust American doctors at all. And it's pretty amazing, because America has fantastic doctors, but for some reason, many of them—they think that the doctors are not particularly competent. . . . See, in Russia the way it was, you go to the doctor and the doctor would spend half an hour talking to you, but they really didn't help you. And here they go to the doctor and the doctor spends two minutes with them. Do you understand?

# Combining Western and Ethnic Folk Medicine

Most participants in the Milwaukee study said they employed a combination of Western and ethnic healthcare approaches. There was no observable pattern in terms of which ethnic groups were more likely to mix the practices. Most of the informants provided pragmatic reasons for their choices.

> *Mexican 174*: We still have our indigenous, wonderful ways of healing. If you go to the Mexican store, you will find lots of herbs. The new generation got divided between using traditional ways and listening to the physicians, who in this country have lost their commitment. In Mexico, you have your personal doctor who cares about you, who is not interested in insurance and costs. Here there are too many steps to get to the physician, which you might not know how to do.

> *Hmong 155*: It's fifty-fifty. I have a grandmother very knowledgeable about herbal meds. Some work. Whatever works. Our people believe in this. We use doctors too. Whatever works.

> *Puerto Rican 184*: There are things people do to complement modern practices. For instance, if you have an infection, you go to the doctor and take the antibiotic. And if you know you have a sore throat, you take rum, lime, and honey.

> *German Russian 165*: They still practice this mystical healing. They have these shamans called *braucheres*. They still practice some sort of mystical healing in the Dakotas and the rural areas and so on. I know people who use this back in the day when their family doctor could not heal them.

> *Chinese 171*: In my instance, I think we were pretty conventional. We follow the Western health methods. We saw the doctor when we were sick. But I do remember the Chinese herbs sitting in jars at home. . . . Though even now if the Western medicine doesn't work, they'll go research the Eastern medicine— what Eastern medicine will work for them. That has also come a long way, I believe. So I wouldn't rule it out.

> *German 140*: The only main difference between German and American healing practices that I can think of is the sauna culture. Germans believe strongly in the preventative and curative properties of both steam and of herbal concoctions. Sauna culture was adopted from the Scandinavian countries, and Germans *love* it, both as a healing practice and a social one. . . . The herbal interest extends in a large way to teas, from chamomile and fennel for belly aches to hibiscus and malt teas for bronchial issues. Healthcare takes place in the home as well as at hospitals.

> *Black Muslim 142*: Many Muslims believe in eating well and don't have any problems with traditional [Western] medicines. There are some older Black Muslims and also some foreign born Muslims who don't trust doctors and the mainstream health practices because of historical government abuse of programs, like the Tuskegee Experiment in the United States and unclean vaccinations that infected many with diseases in other countries. The issue that many Muslims universally have a problem with is treatment for mental health problems. Some people believe that depression can be treated with prayer, for example.

*Chilean 155*: On [name of street], there are [names of two clinics]. And they can work together. They charge based on income, and you can get a massage for one dollar for alternative medicine. They're trying to mix the traditional and alternative medicines to heal. There is a strong belief in cultural healings that Latinos still use. . . . They'll complain about the typical doctors seeing them briefly and formally. Also, many people don't have insurance so they'll try practical ways first, and if it doesn't go away after awhile, then they'll pay.

# Exclusive Use of Ethnic Folk Medicine

Some Milwaukee informants suggested they preferred the folk medicine. Again, there was no ethnic pattern to this choice, and there was much variation in responses within ethnic groups. Some revered the folk remedies because of their spiritual significance and others simply believed in their results.

*African Somali Bantu 191*: We also have *Sharaara* that is played in traditional dance when someone is sick. That is like calling out the devils and giving traditional herbs. Usually it is used by a herbalist. They get branches and roots and cook and crush. They believe that when the person uses that medicine they will get healed. They don't get healed by modern medicine. If they go and play the *Sharaara* and get some traditional medicines they get healed.

*Slovenian 155*: My father was a big believer in home remedies, often involving alcohol. The cure for the common cold or sore throats was brandy, lemon, and honey. Stomachaches were cured with *brinovec*, which derives from the word *brin*, a juniper shrub, and it is made from *brinove jagode*, juniper berries. The people from the old country hated drafts, and had an aversion to excessive air conditioning, which I share. My father thought it was bad to sit on anything cold like a metal folding chair or concrete, and sitting around in a wet swimming suit was especially discouraged. The first thing you drank in the morning had to be hot. Tea, or *chai*, was considered healthy. I grew up drinking tea with caffeine in it early grade school. Chamomile and linden blossom tea were highly respected.

*North American Indian Cree 101*: I'm a spiritual person. The sweat lodge to me is like the womb of mother earth and I'm being washed clean. I am called to help people. I've healed in so many ways and am so thankful for this way of life. There are different types of sweats . . . If a person is sick we have a different ceremony. They all have different instructions from the spirits.

*Bolivian 185*: The indigenous do everything with plants. Their medicine comes from plants. If you have a headache, for example, instead of taking a pill or something, they take coca leaves. They used that for medicine and for religion. And you can also see the future, with *la oja de coca*. That's why the coca is part of our religion.

*Czech 102*: They [Czechs] don't believe in doctors, but they believe in their herbal medicine. I think once I went to the doctor for tonsillitis, but I was eighteen before I went to the doctor.

## The Following Chapter

In chapter 1, ethnicity was defined as follows: "Ethnicity involves biological linkages, shared practices, an element of subjectivity, and unlike many other group memberships, 'is oriented toward the past, toward the history and origin of family, group, and nation'" (Alba, 1990, p. 37). The orientation toward the past is integral to ethnicity. No ethnic practice is as totally oriented toward the past as is genealogy, the subject of chapter 10.

# Chapter Ten
# Ethnic Practices: Genealogy

Any historian or archaeologist can provide a list of reasons why the past matters. People learn from past experiences, individual and collective identities emerge from the past, history helps people understand change, knowledge of the past often makes better citizens, historic conservation preserves cultural forms for the future, and teaching the past elucidates the meanings and values that preceding generations attributed to their heritage (Holtorf, 2012). Salter (2004a) maintains that the search for roots may be part of self-actualization, ala Masloff. And the list goes on.

The practice of genealogy is one way to pursue the past. In the United States, genealogy is a major leisure time activity and has grown exponentially since the advent of the World Wide Web and access to DNA labs ("How Popular," 2009; Kennett, 2011). Genealogy is intrinsically connected to ethnicity, as individuals seeking information on their roots must understand ethnic migration and immigration patterns to locate their ancestors. The website www.cindislist.com has more than 300,000 genealogy links, and approximately one-third of these are to geographic areas and ethnic and subnational groups. Another genealogy website, www.rootsweb.ancestry.com, offers mailing lists for people to share genealogy information. Of the thirty-two thousand plus lists, approximately one-fourth are designated for ethnic and national origins research. Moreover DNA laboratories across the country now offer tests to help people locate relatives. Those that test DNA, such as Family Tree DNA, 23 and Me, and Ancestry, also provide clients with personal percentages of their Asian, African, European (and sometimes Middle Eastern) origins, as well as trace the migration patterns of client matrilineal and patrilineal lines (called haplogroups) over thousands of years.

For some Milwaukee informants, these new developments inspired them to learn new technologies.

*German 120*: In my family there was always a debate over whether or not we had some Jewish ancestors. I was the first one among my cousins to learn how to use the Internet to look for these questionable ancestors, and eventually to do the DNA test. Now the cousins are in agreement that we did really have some Jewish ancestors.

*Scots Irish 146*: Computers scared me. But when people started telling me that I could do much more genealogy on them, I eventually caved in and learned the new technology. Now every day I check some listserv for my ethnic backgrounds or genealogy the first thing when I get up in the morning.

Many participants in the Milwaukee study augmented their ethnic practices with genealogy research. In a few cases, the interest in ethnicity actually followed an interest in genealogy.

*Scots Irish 180*: I guess because my grandfather had an Irish name I just assumed he was Irish, even though it was odd because he was Protestant. But once I got into genealogy a little deeper I learned he was actually Scottish. That led me to the Highland Games [a Scottish event], and the rest is history.

*English 194*: Who would have believed I had Asian Indian blood? When I took the DNA test and they gave me the chart and said I was 12 percent Asian, at first I thought I might be Native American. But I got farther and farther into it and found out that I had a great grandparent who was from India. While I still consider myself English, I am really learning about India now. I plan to take a trip there as soon as I can afford it. I've already made Indian friends and have learned how to make some dishes, like *dosa* and *palak paneer*.

*Kashubian 131*: I didn't even know I was Kashubian until my husband started doing genealogy.

However, for most of the Milwaukee participants, interest in genealogy developed in the context of ethnic pursuits.

## Genealogy as Reverence for Ancestors

Some scholars argue that ancestral reverence played some role in the history of all, or nearly all, cultural groups (Lind, 2007; Steadman, Palmer, and Tilley, 2002). The practice still exists today among a vast number of ethnic groups in Asia, Africa, Oceania, and the Americas (DeVos, 1998; Jellema, 2007; Kendall, 2001; Lee and Sun, 1995; Zuidima, 2003). For many members of these ethnic groups, genealogy is not a pursuit of knowledge of past ancestors, but a permanent record of lineage members who still act in the lives of their descendants. Those in the Milwaukee sample discussed how this practice works.

*Hmong 125*: We believe that people come to this world and when [they] depart go back and be with grandparents and great grandparents. During a funeral we guide the person back step by step.

*North American Indian Lakota 164*: I think the respect for our ancestors and our elders is most important to us. It is part of our spiritual life and our communal life. I do not believe there is a North American Indian tribe that does not revere its ancestors and pay the highest respect to its elders.

*Korean 133*: It's important to me to know my genealogy because traditionally we venerated our ancestors. Even though my family is actually Catholic, we still have rites to our ancestors like remembering our ancestor on the anniversary of his death, the night before. We even have rites for our ancestors way back. So genealogy is important, of course.

# Genealogy as Identity

For those ethnic informants who do not practice ancestral reverence, genealogy became a way to contextualize their own identity. Who were the ancestors? Where did they live? When did they leave their homelands? What was their religious background?

*Scottish 160*: My ancestors came from the area around Beith which is a small town southeast of Glasgow. They owned collieries—coal mines in Scotland—and my grandfather was a graduate civil engineer from the University of Glasgow who immigrated to the US in the 1880s and married in [Wisconsin city], worked as an engineer for the [Name] Machine Company, and raised a large family in [Wisconsin city].

*German 146*: I do know that when my ancestors did settle here in the [Name] township area, that they settled with everyone from the Cologne area. So basically, all the descendents—everybody there—was from Cologne. They just bought the surrounding farmlands, stuff like that, so everyone would have been Roman Catholic. And pretty much they still are. But then you'll see a township right next to it, and they'll be entirely Lutheran. I know that they did stay within their religious group.

*Scots Irish 188*: My ancestors came from Northern Ireland and settled in Appalachia during the early 1700s. I've learned so much about Appalachia and Appalachian life to try and understand what their lives were like.

*Italian 144*: My great, great grandpa came over in 1869. A little bit atypical. They settled out in Minnesota on a farm, as opposed to Milwaukee. Then my grandpa and his brother came over and they lived in Western Wisconsin and came to the Milwaukee area in the late forties to establish the construction company which they started in 1954, and so the family has been in the area ever since. So we're a little bit atypical. My ancestors came from a larger town. Its [name of town] which is just southeast of Genoa. So that's that.

The following example from field notes helps demonstrate the intensity of the interest in genealogy among one ethnic group.

*Field notes: February, 2001*
[I'd been the principal investigator on the Milwaukee ethnic studies project for about a year, and our first product was a documentary on the Irish that settled in one Milwaukee neighborhood.] A woman called me saying that she was from a group of Milwaukee Irish genealogists and asked if I could come to her meeting and show and discuss the new documentary. I said this could be done and asked if they had a VCR available. She assured me that the group had a "very large screen VCR player."

I had visualized sitting around a table of five or six genealogists having an intimate chat on our ongoing Irish study, and then introducing the documentary. I had prepared no formal presentation. As I arrived at the community center, the woman led me through the back door, down a series of hallways, and then to a room where she showed me the controls to this "very large" VCR. "But where's the screen?" I asked. The woman then escorted me out of the room onto a stage in an auditorium. "It's here," she answered, pointing to a screen the size of a child's bedroom wall. I gasped as I looked out onto the auditorium floor and saw people beginning to fill nearly one hundred of the seats.

Somehow I stumbled through an ad lib presentation that introduced the video, followed by an hour of discussion. I was still learning about ethnicity in Milwaukee, but it was the last time I ever underestimated the level of participation in ethnic activities.

# Genealogy as Appreciation for Sacrifice

A number of participants in the Milwaukee study discussed ways that genealogy helped them value their own lives more after learning the difficult conditions their ancestors endured. Some expressed appreciation for the sacrifices their ancestors made.

*Dutch 102*: You look at all these death certificates you collect. This one dies of pneumonia, that one from TB, and one actually died because of a cut on the ankle that apparently wouldn't heal and became septic. All this was before there were antibiotics. I sometimes just sit and wonder how much you would have worried back then when you know you have some infection. You have to ask: "Is this it for me?" Worse yet if it was one of your kids.

*African Somali Bantu 192*: We are the slave descendants of [Zanzibar slave trade]. . . . The country is Somalia and the people that live there are Somalis and we are not Somalis, but because we lived in that country that is how we are Somali Bantu. It is not our original country. Then came the civil war in that country, which is how we ended up here.

*Jewish 115*: My Jewish ancestors came from Russia in the 1880s due to the pogroms they faced. The Jewish Alliance helped. The move was so hard because they left everything they loved to come here, but had they not come, of course I would not be here—I mean literally—alive. My siblings would not be here. My cousins would not be here.

*English 199*: You look at their wills [ancestors]. You almost cry. All that was written by hand and witnessed and it amounted to some cooking pot, a table, a mare, and two sets of clothes. I try and imagine what life was like for the frontier people and how hard they struggled, having to move on all the time when they couldn't get a crop. And those wills. An entire life spent and they left a pot to a daughter, the mare to the spouse, the table to a son, and the clothes to whoever they fit. That's the entire life and probably as much as they ever owned. But they left kids behind. They managed to raise them until they were old enough to start their own families. And out of all that came us. I look at what I own—maybe thirty outfits, two cars, a house, furniture in every room, a ton of technology, and so on. But now, when I start to think my life has not yielded much, I go back to those wills. And I still tear up.

*Russian 121*: But, I think that many Americans still think that in World War II the United States fought Russia and its ally, Hitler. So, the reality is not well known among more Americans. . . . Now it's amazing, they're making so sophisticated movies about what has actually happened in World War II. How simple people like in my family suffered, and what kind of sacrifice was extorted from the nation in order to beat fascism.

*Swedish 116*: I would like to say certain Lutheran congregations—that they certainly sacrificed to construct [them] in turn of the century times. And certainly those buildings are great historical and cultural remnants of Scandinavian American past. I am not so sure that those congregations are much a part of the Scandinavian present. My sense is that Scandinavians really have scattered, maybe even more so than most all European ethnics in Milwaukee, far and wide throughout greater Milwaukee and there isn't much of that concentration of Scandinavians left at this point. But someone still appreciates the sacrifice of those great buildings.

## The Following Chapter

Genealogy helped many Milwaukee informants ground themselves to the past and have a better understanding of what their ethnic groups experienced and contributed to American life. Genealogy often helped them form a more substantive *civic* identity. What they did with that civic identity is discussed in chapter 11 on political activity.

# Chapter Eleven
# Ethnic Practices: Political Activity

Much of the ethnic literature in the middle of the twentieth century focused on the role of ethnicity in competition for power and resources (Barth, 1966; Bell, 1975; A. Cohen, 1974a; Despres, 1975; Glazer and Moynihan, 1970). This was a major argument of the instrumentalist point of view outlined in chapter 1, where ethnic factions were portrayed as pressure groups vying for political muscle. In the United States, some of the potential for ethnic power was mitigated by the passage of the Civil Service Reform Act of 1978 which created the US Merit Systems Protection Board. This quasi-judicial agency was established to protect federal merit systems against prohibited personnel practices and to ensure protection for federal employees against abuses by agency management. This meant that an agency that was managed by a member of one ethnic group could not specifically commit promotions and important positions to members of the same group, as had often been the case in the past. While the progression of ethnic political patronage slowed, some groups remained more successful than others in clearing the path to political success.

## Unequal Access to Political Power

As in many US cities, the Milwaukee Irish found avenues to political power. Andrew Greeley (1981), who studied the Irish for decades, documents Irish achievement in political life. In the Milwaukee study, a number of Irish informants discussed the strategies involved in this success.

> *Irish 185*: Children were involved with politics. My father would get us involved. He'd pick a candidate and give us a reason for wanting this candidate to win the election. We'd work for the candidate, handing out literature, whatever was needed.

*Irish 135*: The unions were very powerful and we hung out in certain bars. We used to decide everything in the bar—who would get this job and that job, who would run for this or that office, how we would get people jobs at the county.

*Irish 158*: The Irish really voted, and often as a block. Politicians would have to cater to us to get our vote. We also had the highest number of people in office.

*Irish 180*: In one neighborhood where so many of us Irish had grown up, there ended up in one fifty-year span [being] over one hundred government department heads, judges, and agency heads. Three of four heads of county government came from this neighborhood.

*Irish 106*: Because we had so many people in office, a lot of people in [name of former Irish neighborhood] relied on public jobs. The news would get passed around on jobs and contracts and what vending lists to get on.

For other groups, accessing the political process was more challenging. Some groups expressed concerns that their small numbers in Milwaukee County left them without adequate representation.

*Luxembourger 102*: You'd be hard pressed to find many Luxembourgers in Milwaukee County. If you drive just a few miles out of Milwaukee and get to [name of town], one out of every two people will claim Luxembourgish ancestry. They have their own museum there. They really get the attention of the elected representatives. Not here.

*Kashubian 134*: We just blend in with the Poles, I suppose, even though we have our own ancestry and a very distinct history in Milwaukee—particularly if you are talking about the Kashubes of Jones Island and the fishing village. But we don't have a voting bloc that can make waves like the Poles have done in the past. There have been times when this might have helped—when we were evicted from the island or when they proposed building a park for us.

A. Smith (1981) claims that ethnic organizing to combat exploitation and inequality is critical for groups at the poverty line. Recent national elections suggest that ethnic identity—particularly Latino identity—is re-emerging as a strong influence on outcomes (Kopicki and Irving, 2012; Vigil, 2012). In the Milwaukee study, informants of less affluent groups were more likely to complain about lack of voting and organizing around issues than others.

*North American Indian Ojibwe 521*: [There's] not enough political activity. It's a personal disappointment. We tried to get voter registration but there was so much disenchantment with government.

*North American Indian Stockbridge Munsee 177*: Years ago there used to be some efforts to court politicians. The mayor was willing to make a commitment to turn over the campus to us, and then wrote a memo against it. I know all my representatives and none of them are aware of Native American issues. We need an educational move that will go and work with these people with a packet of info. They have no idea there's Indians in an urban environment.

*Puerto Rican 132*: In Puerto Rico, they are very involved in politics. Around election time, it looks like a parade, because the political parties are so organized. There are rallies in every single *pueblo,* and so there is a lot of involvement. Here, we don't vote. Latinos are one of the lowest voting groups. Well, with some Mexicans and the rest of Latin America, they don't have the legal status to vote, but Puerto Ricans can, and still don't. We have to change the apathy. It's a self-fulfilling prophecy—the system is not working for me, so there is no use voting. Without realizing it's not working for you because you aren't voting.

*African American 190*: I am disappointed by this. The percentage that vote is low. Our school board races are embarrassingly low. You can get elected with four hundred votes. I'd like to see more education done in schools on citizenship.

*Hmong 122*: But our needs are still underserved. Hmong still have to learn how to use [the] system to their advantage—we don't know how. If they do know about it they are intimidated and don't know how to advocate for themselves. They have been passive.

In the following example from field notes—taken about three years after most Hmong were interviewed—the Hmong begin to make their issues (and their presence) more public.

*Field Notes: April, 2008*
Up to two hundred Hmong were rallying on the plaza at City Hall this morning. The demonstration had been announced days earlier, and it was in response to a police beating of a Hmong man who had been confronted by police. The police claimed the man was stopped for suspicion of drunken driving and tried to flee, but the Hmong community had been insisting this was an issue of lack of interpreters and knowledge of Hmong culture at the Milwaukee Police Department. A TV camera was present and a Hmong leader was being interviewed.

A crowd of onlookers had gathered. A man to my left leaned in my direction. "I don't get it," he mumbled.

"It's about a man being beaten by police," I offered.

"Well, I can read the signs. But who are *they*?"

"The Hmong."

"Spell it."

"H-m-o-n-g. They're Southeast Asians."

"Oh, I've seen that name before, but I thought it was pronounced with an H. I didn't know what they were." He hesitated. "Okay. So I learned something."

# Issues Involving Past Homelands

A common concern among many Milwaukee groups was advocating for policies that would favor past homelands and (where applicable) ease immigration restrictions from these areas.

*Arab 122*: Politics? That's all we talk about. . . . International politics is always a topic of discussion among Arabs. You can't go into any gathering and have someone not talking about international politics. I think that has to do with the conflicts in the Middle East and United States foreign policy. So that's always a discussion. In terms of national politics, I think more and more over the years, the Arab community has gotten more involved and more active. I think there's been a realization that in order for there to be a change, or for an individual or group to influence their elected official, they need to get involved and have a voice. You'll see many individuals in the community hosting fundraisers for the elected officials.

*Mexican 114*: We always have the same trouble. Immigration is the most important reason keeping us together. We have people living in this country with no documents and no rights, and yet have all the responsibilities of paying taxes, and making this country rich. . . . In-state tuition fees are another issue. It is difficult for an undocumented child, having no social security number, to pay for school. Instead of three thousand dollars per year, it will be thirteen thousand dollars. It makes it impossible. You are being denied. Then after all the years of going to high school without any documents, they know that they will not be able to go to college. If you see how bad Latinos are doing in the education area, it is because of that. They are smart and they know there is no way they can go to college. They drop out of high school more than any other group—more than African Americans, Native Americans. Why? Because they know they are not going to college . . . having lived in this country for many years, with their parents paying taxes all these years. We need the legislature to stop this.

*Jewish 116*: You see extreme views among Jews, I think. You have the founders of socialism and communism, and their backbone parties, being Jewish. Then you had some rabbis that joined the Moral Majority in the late eighties. I think that many, perhaps most, will vote based on Israeli issues.

*African Somali 108*: Most of the citizens of Africa origin vote, you know, and their concerns are not different than that of average American, who are concerned about war, healthcare, you know, economy, and they also like to see a close ties with Africa. They'd like to see United States having close ties with Africa.

*African Kenya Mbere 181*: At the same time we follow the American politics—especially the controversial issue about immigration reform. That is something that we are talking about. Of course we express our own political opinions about what is going on in American politics. Not just immigration but in general who we see as being more migrant friendly, the Republicans or the Democrats. We follow both the politics of here and Kenya.

## The Following Chapter

Scholars writing in the instrumentalist school of thought usually tied political power to various economic pursuits, such as competition for jobs. This author has reserved the economic findings for last, because of some of the interesting and unexpected findings that emerged under the category. For example, this was the only topic where informants elected to compare the practices of the early generations of their ethnic group in America to later generations. Read on in chapter 12.

# Chapter Twelve
# Ethnic Practices: Working

Recently a caller on a radio talk show in Milwaukee asked this question: "Why can't immigrants be like they used to be? Those Europeans that came here back in the day really knew how to work." The complaint is one heard often on the streets of Milwaukee (and probably elsewhere in the United States as well). The assumption seems to be that any ethnic group that arrived in large numbers in the late twentieth century—especially if the group was comprised of people of color—was more of a drain on the US economy than a contributor. Per Jacobson (2006, p. 353), the fables of bootstrapping among white-only immigrants was based on centuries of "political culture, where, by myth, legend, and impressive consensus, the word 'immigrant' has long meant 'European.'"

And the issue gets hotter. The news in 2012 that the number of non-white babies born in the United States had outstripped the number of white babies spurred heated blog activity on the Internet. The development had been projected since the 1970s, in part because of US policies. Government policies always played a major role in the ethnic makeup of nations (Hoddie, 2006). In the United States, the legislation that had the greatest impact on national ethnic composition was the Immigration and Nationality Act of 1965, or the Hart-Celler Act. Between 1920 and 1965, legal immigration averaged approximately 206,000 people per year. Before 1965, immigrants came to America for a variety of reasons, and most of these came from Northern Europe. In 1921, the United States guaranteed that this trend would continue—at least for a time. Addressing the fear that America was becoming more diverse, Congress passed the 1921 Emergency Quota Law. The objective of this act was to impose quotas based on the country of birth. Annual allowable quotas for each country were calculated at 3 percent of the total number of foreign-born people from that country in the 1910 US census. This meant that 70 percent of all immigrants in the immediate future would come from Great Britain, Ireland, and Germany. The ethnic status quo was ensured—at least until 1965.

The passage of the 1965 legislation changed the volume and origins of immigrants by discontinuing quotas based on national origins and giving preference to those with US relatives. This ended the preference for Northern

European immigrants. By the 1980s the non-white population was growing seven times faster than whites. The combination of the new immigration policy, illegal immigration, and high birth rates of the new immigrants altered the national demographic to the extent that by the middle of the twenty-first century, *most adult Americans* will have African, Asian, Latin American, Pacific Island, or Arab ancestry (Schaefer, 2007; Waller, 2000; Yang, 1995).

But the demographic changes say nothing about the working lives of the new immigrants. Considerable scholarly literature on immigrants and their offspring has focused on whether they gained socioeconomic status and education over time and the ways that earning a living changed or failed to change in succeeding generations (Farley and Alba, 2002; Feliciano, 2006; Gans, 1992; Gold, 2006; Zhou, 1997). The assumption in the literature has been that immigrants (and in some cases migrants) and their children are successful if they ultimately gain wealth, professional status, and advanced degrees comparable to long-established populations. However, most of the studies cited in these sources also indicate that socioeconomic mobility of immigrants/migrants and their descendants is tied to the conditions of the families *before* they arrived at their destinations and the opportunities they faced in America. The families that came from wealth and privilege—those who arrived with material and *social* capital—were more likely to succeed than the families that came from poverty. Race also played a key role, if it translated into denied opportunities of some groups in America. Very little in the literature speaks about the relative work ethic of immigrant or migrant groups—*a trait they all can possess.*

In the Milwaukee study, the effects of socioeconomic advantages and opportunities on immigrant/migrant mobility were clearly supported by informant stories. But informants also discussed attendant issues related to their early-arriving families, such as the context of the initial settlement and the work ethic of the immigrant/migrant generation. These topics are discussed in the following sections where the European and non-European accounts are compared.

# Reasons for Immigration/Migration

Ancestors of the Milwaukee informants left their homelands for most of the reasons that others did. Access to land, jobs, and more political and religious freedoms in America were always pull factors drawing immigrants and migrants. Chief push factors cited by the Milwaukee informants included religious and political persecution; forced emigration (e.g., slavery, indentured servitude, prisoner deportations); the Irish potato famine and other crop failures; the 1848 collapse of democratic revolutions in Europe; civil wars or wars of occupation; conscription; low wages and unemployment; the Industrial Revolution upsetting fragile peasant lifestyles; reunification with families in America (especially after 1965); and refugee status.

Among those who had oral or written accounts of their first ancestors in Milwaukee County, or those who had been immigrants/migrants themselves, over three-quarters discussed profound hardships and suffering just before they arrived. The European and non-European informants shared similar stories.

*Irish 196*: My family was literally starving [because of the potato famine]. The family that came here—my ancestors—had already lost three kids by the time they got on the boat and lost two more on the journey here.

*African Congo Congolese 172*: I was involved in Congo political activity. I was a strong supporter of democracy in my country. I had a very loyal family who protected me but I had to flee to a different country because members of the government were looking for her [me?]. I was on a plane in South Africa and I was told to remove myself from the plane by the pilot because people were looking for me. I had to beg him to let me stay. Through the US I came to New York City even though I wanted to come to Canada. When I arrived at the immigration office no one spoke French, and I spoke no English. It took some time to find someone who spoke French. My children at the immigration office were socializing the officer even though they did not speak the same language. Yet they got along together. With help from the immigration officer that met my children we were able to come to Milwaukee and find a place to stay.

*Italian 124*: Well, actually my grandfather had a cousin who had immigrated to Milwaukee earlier. And because of the economic climate in Sicily, and the political social climate in Sicily, in the twenties when Mussolini was in power, my grandfather had to leave Sicily. He was a Socialist and they were not popular with Mussolini, so he had an opportunity to come here, and his sponsor was just a cousin in Milwaukee, and he came to Milwaukee, liked it, felt it had better opportunities for himself and his family and subsequently moved the family over here, so it was political, economic, and social.

*African South Togo Mina 101*: [My family members] came here for political reasons. There are embassies over there that help them to get here and get refugee. They run away from killing people who want to kill their families. If they survive they come here to survive, to get away from all that killing and treachery.

*German 183*: [My mother] was a refugee from East Germany. The East German police pistol whipped her, broke her jaw, and told her to come back in the evening, and everyone knows what that means.

*Hmong 130*: During the [Vietnam] War my dad was a war captain. He worked with the CIA to fight against communists from North [Vietnam] to Laos to South Vietnam. When Laos fell in 1975, he feared persecution. The Hmong were threatened with extermination. We went to Thailand. We were six months in Thailand in a refugee camp [before coming to the United States].

*Russian Jewish 181*: On my father's side was a town near Kiev. And my grandfather and his cousin went out hunting one day. And while they were gone—I don't know if it was more than a day or two—but their entire village was killed by a pogrom that came through. Everyone was killed and they were the only two survivors of their village. . . . And on my mother's side, my great grandparents were kicked out of Russia, and went to Poland. And my grandparents were born in Poland. And then they were kicked out of Poland, and then they went on to Israel. And so my mother was born in Israel and immigrated to the United States in 1948.

*African American 110*: My great grandfather came up from Mississippi where they were literally starving on a rented piece of land, and where Jim Crow was the order of the day. He heard about jobs here, came up, then after he got a job, brought up the rest of his family.

For those who finally made it to Milwaukee, life became less challenging, but only slightly so.

# Getting Established

Niche has always played a role in the settlement of immigrants and migrants, especially in urban areas such as Milwaukee County. Ethnic niches in employment usually proceed through known opportunities passed on by networks of families and former neighbors. But the groups still need to accept the opportunities, and the choice of work had to suit their cultural preferences and experiences (Wallman, 1979). Many immigrants gravitate toward self-employment— sometimes to fill a need in their own ethnic group, but also because other job avenues have been denied (Jenkins, 1984).

The Milwaukee informants discussed their economic survival in the area. Here the Europeans will be compared to the non-Europeans.

## The Europeans

Some typical niches for European immigrants in the United States had been foundries and mills for Slovenians, shopkeeping and the garment industry for Russian and Polish Jews, food service for Greeks, fishing for Portuguese, steelmaking and coal mining for Poles, and building trades and barber shops for Italians (Noble, 1992). In the Milwaukee study, European informants discussed the reciprocal nature of getting established in America. While most talked about the reasons the immigrant generation had to leave past homelands or the desire for new opportunities in America, they also discussed the ways that the immigrant generation inhabited niches that needed filling in America. At times ethnic group members already possessed the skills to fill a previously defined niche, while others took jobs that no one else wanted. Still others had actually been *recruited* by Americans from their past homeland to fill available jobs.

*Norwegian 130*: My immigrant ancestors. You know Norwegians are well known for cutting stone. And also they were very good at climbing. They were the ones, when there were building tall buildings, they used to climb up there and stuff like that. That goes way back.

*Polish 138*: My great grandfather came as a glass blower. This was a Polish niche mainly, and Milwaukee was glad to have him.

*Irish 136*: Those of us that first settled in the East pretty much built the eastern section of the transcontinental railroad. It was dangerous work, and barely no one else wanted it. We continued working for the railroad as we moved west, and we really did this in [name of Milwaukee neighborhood], where the railroad shops hired some two thousand people, or perhaps more.

*German 121*: Well, historically, there was quite a distinction between the farmers and the crafts people. Most of the Germans were farmers and they settled throughout the state [of Wisconsin]. Then, in specific craft areas, you found [German] people very skilled in the brewing industry, very skilled in the tanning business. . . . I might add also, the later waves of [German] immigration presented people in the printing and machine tool and die business.

*Greek 113*: My father, who was much older than my mother, came in the early part of the twentieth century to work for a factory in [town near Milwaukee]. The recruiting company would send representatives to Italy and Greece and would recruit entire villages. Most young men from the villages all came together and settled in [town near Milwaukee] and Milwaukee. So there's lots of Greeks from the same villages that ended up here.

*Scottish 150*: The immigrants generally who directly came from Scotland were basically people who were recruited to come as craftsmen and workers of that sort in Milwaukee. A lot of them worked at a company called [name of company] and a lot of them worked at a company called—it just jumped out of my head. By then they would come and work as, you know, as tool and die makers—things of that sort. People with skilled trades of that sort so that was the basic way in which most of them made their living.

## The Non-Europeans

The same patterns held true for the non-Europeans in the Milwaukee study. They described their immigrant/migrant ancestors as occupying niches that needed to be filled, working jobs no one else wanted, or having been recruited from their former homes to fill jobs in America.

*Arab 116*: We were good tradesmen and I think there was this need for this back when my grandparents settled here. We opened the carpet stores and the little grocers in neighborhoods where they were needed.

*Pakistani 177*: My family came to open a gas station. A lot of Indians and Pakistanis and I guess Russians and I guess other immigrants have stations here in this town. You don't see many other people owning them.

*African American 191*: My ancestors in the South were metal workers—a skill they brought with them from Africa, I am told. I think we [African Americans] have more day care centers than anyone else. My family was involved in this since we came up from the South. It used to be we'd be hired to live in white people's houses to be nannies. Today all the women work and they need this. It's like you can't have enough childcare. You see a new one opening every day.

*Hmong 101*: My dad works cleaning asbestos out of buildings. This is not a great job and we worry about him. A lot of Hmong got jobs doing this. It has to be done.

*Chinese 189*: Most of my ancestors went to the West Coast originally to—well, you'll think this is silly—to mine gold. Except the gold rush was dead by the time they got there. They then had the chance to work on the transcontinental railroad and did this. But it was very dangerous and they were happy to move on to different things. But they built most of the western part of this railroad and are just now getting credit for this.

*African American 169*: My grandparents came up here from Mississippi in the 1940s. I was told that they'd been recruited by the factories and brought up by them—brought up in boxcars, not passenger cars. I guess the companies needed workers because of the war. The men came first, to work in the factories. We lived around [street name] until they razed that area, due to the freeway. Most of the men and a lot of the women worked in the factories in the [Milwaukee area] and some on the north side. There was a lot of work then.

*Mexican 120*: My grandfather was brought up from Mexico with others from his village to break a strike at [Milwaukee company]. But they didn't know they were breaking a strike. They were just told that they had an opportunity to work for higher wages than they had back home. So that's how my family ended up here.

The following example from field notes shows ways that some Hmong found a niche that was both needed in Milwaukee and helped them maintain cultural practices.

*Field Notes: August, 2009*
Unlike his mother, "Xang" spoke perfect English. He helped her load and unload vegetables on Sunday morning. After setting up the tent, Xang took all the produce from the back of the family pickup truck and organized the vegetable display for the farmers' market. His mother moved around the cabbage and radishes and straightened out the rows. Xang's eight-year-old son, who spoke both Hmong and English, was chubby by Hmong standards. He helped his family with the markets and in exchange collected a few quarters.

The market organizer apologized to Xang because the crowds had been sparse lately. Xang said it didn't matter. These were vegetables left over from their Saturday market and he was glad to have a place to sell them. He said his mother did most of the gardening on rented plots owned by the [name of program] in her own Milwaukee neighborhood. The gardening helped her maintain Hmong cultural traditions. She could plant the kinds of vegetables they used for cooking Hmong dishes and also reap a few medicinal herbs. The farmers' markets had been wonderful niches for the Hmong in Milwaukee to sell off their surplus. Very few farmers from the rural areas were willing to drive fifty miles to the city to service these venues.

Xang had a job for a nonprofit. He was born in a refugee camp in Thailand, came to the United States at age eight, learned English, and later earned a degree in social welfare. He explained that his parents' generation had a hard time learning English because the Hmong written language was a relatively new development and few members of the older generation knew it back in Laos. This made learning a new language very difficult. He was just happy his mother was able to keep busy with gardening and keep the Hmong culinary traditions alive.

When the tent was completely organized, Xang left his mother and son to sell their produce. While Xang's son could do translations, most of the time the grandmother was able to negotiate sales through hand gestures. Within minutes she was busy taking orders. The boy was off buying Tootsie Rolls from other vendors with the quarters he'd earned.

# Effects of Deindustrialization

Every generation of immigrants or migrants faced their own challenges when they arrived at their destination. The late twentieth century offered its own challenges. The deindustrialization of the 1980s had altered the economic landscape. For example, villagers that had been recruited from Mexico early in the century to work in the foundries and tanneries in Milwaukee would no longer find available factory work in the 1990s. Those of any ethnic background without formal educations might end up in temporary employment or low-paying jobs in the service industry.

*Puerto Rican 104*: Then there was the era where factory jobs, especially in Milwaukee, were the primary source of employment. So my grandfather found employment in a factory and all the children were brought over. That's the general pattern. Heavier migration started in the fifties and sixties as migrant farm workers who were later transferred to the factories. The jobs didn't pay much, but it was still better than what they were being paid in their home countries. Decline in factory jobs caused Puerto Ricans to slide down the economic ladder. Many of the jobs that men traditionally had have disappeared. The jobs remaining are the social service jobs that are mostly done by women. My grandfather, for instance, has been working in the same factory for thirty years. When he lost his job, there was not much else he could do.

*Mexican 114*: Many people traditionally earned their living in the manufacture [sic] industry. The Midwest was once called the "Rust Belt" because of all the manufacture jobs. There are some in the service industry, and also organizations such as this—white-collar jobs. There are an awful lot in the universities, in the school system, and in some corporations. So there is a whole spectrum now, from entry-level jobs to white-collar jobs. Very diverse. In the beginning, however, twenty-five to thirty years ago, most people were either in the factories or the service industries, which is common when new people are coming into the geographic area, whether they were Mexican, Cuban, or the Irish, or Germans, or whatever the case may be. Once they settled, they went through a transformation of sorts. They begin to establish themselves.

*Polish 144*: [When I immigrated in the 1990s], all I could get was temporary jobs—get up early in the morning and take buses with those Mexican guys to go to some job for that day and [a] couple more. Then a painter hired me and they all spoke Polish. But I still can't make enough to live.

*Chilean 152*: Factories are moving out of Milwaukee and going abroad to save money, pollute in other countries like Mexico, etcetera. The growth of the labor agencies I think are a crime because the factories are not hiring directly anymore. They hire from the labor agencies. Why? Because they will prove [that] workers are replaceable. They don't pay any kind of insurance. I've seen many workers that have lost their fingers, etcetera, and nobody will cover them because there is no documentation. Also I see workers that won't go to labor agencies and will be on the corner, and construction companies will pick them up, have them work, but not pay them.

The next section will present findings on work ethics of the immigrant or migrant generation and subsequent generations.

# Work Ethics

In an article comparing native American and immigrant workers, Roger Waldinger (1997, p. 376) excerpts an interview from an employer of both.

Yes, the immigrants just want to work, work long hours, just want to do anything. They spend a lot of money coming up from Mexico. They want as many hours as possible. If I called them in for 4 [sic] hours to clean latrines, they'd do it. They like to work. They have large families, a big work ethic, and small salaries. The whites have more, so they're willing to work fewer hours. Vacation time is important to them. They get a play and want to get two months off. They want me to rearrange a schedule at a moment's notice. These guys in the back would never dream of that. They would like to go back to Mexico every four years for a month which I [let them] do. The back of the house workers take vacation pay and then work through their vacations. I try to get them to take off a week once a year. But most of them plead poverty. The kids [who are natives] in the front of the house are still being taken care of by their parents. I'm not trying to disparage them, but they're spoiled.

This contrast between native-born Americans and newly arrived immigrants and migrants came up often during interviews in the Milwaukee study. While the interview guide posed no specific questions on generations or work ethic, the informants volunteered a lot of information on both topics.

## The Europeans

The European American informants stressed the hardships and struggles that their immigrant generation had endured in America, and the sacrifices that generation made for their children.

> *German 113*: My grandfather was always so proud of the fact that by the time that he came to America to the time he retired, he never missed a day of work. There was never a day he didn't work. That was typical in the German community. Nobody wanted to miss a day of work.

> *Kashubian 134*: Their main occupation was fishing. They'd get up at three or four in the morning, be out on the lake and not come back until early afternoon. Then they'd work at the dock for three or four hours, cleaning and drying fish and the nets. They wanted the kids to have something better.

> *Greek 153*: Back in the old days they were known to have shoe-shines [and] lots and lots of restaurants, grocery stores, [and] one of the more visible ethnic groups in the restaurant business. Education for the kids was so stressed. It was encouraged to be better than your parents.

> *Norwegian 115*: I think that there were people that when they came over here, they learned to work in the factories and whatever skills because most of them that came over here came from rural communities and so their skill was farming and keeping the land, but they learned. . . . When my spouse's mother came, she worked as a domestic. But I think there were many people, particularly women, who worked as domestics.

Many of those interviewed spent time reflecting on the immigrant work practices they'd just discussed and questioned whether these were still the norm. Most conceded that jobs were easier today, but they also expressed concerns that the work ethic had waned in succeeding generations.

> *Scots Irish 190*: I think the jobs are easier now, especially with computers. I don't know that anyone really gets into any backbreaking jobs, except if you are in construction or cleaning. There aren't many Scots Irish in Milwaukee, but those I know work mainly in nice offices.

*Polish 166*: The next generations didn't work as hard as the immigrants. I would say not. They didn't have as much to prove and the struggle wasn't as hard. No language to learn, no new rules. Most of us [in later generations] had never experienced much hardship.

*German 169*: Germans always took pride in our work ethic. It was a work ethic for its own sake, not just so we'd climb up in some job. This is not what it once was. Germans have become a lot like other Americans and the work ethic is diminished.

*Russian 150*: Do the young people today struggle like their parents did? No. I guess they just don't have much to prove. They know they have the support.

*Kashubian 110*: It used to be that we were called hard workers but also hard partiers. Maybe today it's more the latter.

## The Non-Europeans

The non-Europeans in the Milwaukee study discussed similar experiences. They lauded the struggles and motivation of the immigrant/migrant generation, often a very recent one. They discussed the desires of their ancestors to improve the quality of life for the children.

*African Congo Congolese 102*: We [immigrant generation] learn English, find a job, and try to continue our education. It is important to become more educated and support our families. As soon as we get to America, we work.

*Palestinian 132*: When my father came he was a tradesperson. Of course we didn't know much English, so he worked in sanitation and in a bakery. As soon as he could afford it, he bought properties and rented them. Then he bought a corner store. But he didn't want us to do that. It was a lot of hard work. . . . But as an immigrant mentality, you do what you can, you get educated, and then you do better. . . . We struggle with that, because sometimes as people from different countries, we have to prove our abilities.

*Mexican 127*: My father could barely understand English but he worked full time and overtime as a janitor in a hotel. He bought this truck and carried loads for people as a free-lancer whenever he had the chance. This money he put away for us. When I went into business he took that money out of the account and gave it to me so I could start a bakery.

*Bulgarian Turk 120*: [An immigrant] Most important [is] that my daughter lives at home and establishes herself before she moves out to get married. I pay her rent and food, and student loans, so I sacrifice to work for us. I don't let my daughter pay for any bills. I pay for books, everything for her. I want her to be established and successful. She appreciates me, so she works very hard in college. She will be the most accomplished chemist in the world! Since she was four years old, she was learning English in Bulgaria. I paid her one dollar for every "A" she got. I am broke now!

*Indian 170*: [An immigrant] Other Indians? From our state, Punjab, they are mostly in the gas stations. So that's mostly what Punjabi people do. Other people, they do Yellow Cab. I mostly came here to buy a gas station with other guys. It didn't work out so then I started searching for a job.

*Chinese 111*: It was just my grandfather [at first]. At that time, women were not following their husbands. Then he started his business as a laundry man right in Milwaukee. He made a successful business of it, supported his family, and I think he sent money back periodically and eventually my dad joined him. My dad took over his business when [my grandfather] passed away and then we started a restaurant in the 1970s. I had helped run that. I think that's a situation where many first-generation immigrants . . . have to help their parents. I hear many stories: "Oh, yeah, I had to do all the work after school. We could not go anywhere." I think that was pretty much the case with us. I was a little older already. I had finished high school and was just starting college, but it did influence my lifestyle because, you know, you just have more of a work ethic, and you didn't really know anything else.

Also similar to the European American informants, many non-Europeans discussed the change in the work ethic over succeeding generations.

*Chinese 179*: But with the next generation, I think there's hardly any pressure on them to do anything. Children were not encouraged to follow their parents' footsteps in those days. They just wanted us to have a better life, get our education, and improve.

*Hmong 122*: It's hard to get your kids really into work. They think because they are an American, [they] don't have to work that hard now.

*African American 112*: Kids today don't know what those early blacks went through coming from the South. They didn't work eight-hour days. They worked until the job was done. Today I have kids—kids that should have jobs—coming here to do gardening and after an hour they ask if that's it. They just broke a sweat.

*Mexican 151*: When my husband and I came up from Mexico, we'd do just about anything. He worked hard construction. I worked cleaning. I don't want to say bad about my kids and grandchildren, but it's not the same now. You know. We made sure our daughter got a college education. She's always had good jobs, but she won't work for what we did. You know. My granddaughter wouldn't take a job in high school or college because she said the pay wasn't good enough. It's just different. Things change.

What are the implications of these findings? What do these and other practices contribute to US collectivities?

## The Following Chapter

A summary and interpretation of the results on working, as well as other ethnic practices, will be presented in chapter 13.

# Chapter Thirteen
# The Sum of Ethnic Practices

An advantage of qualitative research is its potential to elucidate the depth and breadth of phenomena under investigation (Denzin and Lincoln, 2005). The findings presented in chapters 3 through 12 were *intended* to be encyclopedic to show the scope of ethnic practices—their meanings, the effects the practices had on the lives of participants—and to put them on display in the words of the ethnic informants themselves. As outlined in the introductory chapter, the older literature focused on ways that retaining ethnic identity and practices benefited (or failed to benefit) *individuals*, most often because ethnicity enhanced affective ties to a population or became a vehicle for organizing economic and political self-interests. These benefits lingered with ethnic Milwaukeeans in the twenty-first century through the vast inventory of leisure time activities that participants could draw on and the economic and political functions of many ethnic organizations. But what was also stated in chapter 1 is that the Milwaukee study demonstrates benefits to collectivities to which individuals belong.

The first and most obvious of these is the family.

## Benefits to Families

When looking back at the practices discussed by the Milwaukee informants, it is difficult to find any that did not include the entire nuclear family and at times the extended family. How often, for example, would parents attend a Kwanza celebration, a powwow, *Festa Italiana*, a *Cinco de Mayo* parade, or the Scottish Highland Games without their children? Ethnic arts such as rosemaling, Hmong story cloths, pasta making, and Indian beading are passed on through families. Genealogy, as a practice, is the celebration of the family, the extended family, and the lineage.

But *wider* collectivities also accrue benefits from ethnic practices.

# Benefits to Wider Collectivities

Collectivities beyond one's family and known lineage can include the neighborhood, organizations, town, nation, and beyond. Ethnic practices add many benefits to the wider collectivities such as enriching the population, adding voluntary associations, illuminating the past, and filling niches.

## Enriching the Population

As has been mentioned several times in this book, ethnicity has been changing. Ethnic involvement is far more subjective and voluntary in the early twenty-first century than it was in the middle of the twentieth century. Individuals today tend to select activities that interest them and enhance the quality of their lives. More often than not, these are enrichment practices—practices that educate or boost a desirable quality.

In the Milwaukee study, informants described a range of enrichments they reaped from their routine ethnic involvement. Some of these included:

- An enhanced knowledge of history, often extending beyond the history of past homelands
- Proficiency in languages other than English
- Involvement in visual, performance, and culinary arts
- Travel
- Knowledge of a body of healing practices and preventive health measures such as saunas, foods, and herbs
- Participation in sports and other health-promoting physical activities

The sum of these endeavors potentially leads to a more educated, cultivated, and healthy American population. Add to this the variety of menus, art forms, dress styles, literature traditions, and music genres (to name just a few) that ethnic practices generally contribute to American life, and the result is more enriched families, neighborhoods, and municipalities.

But there are other ways that ethnic practices enhance collectivities.

## Added Voluntary Associations

In 1835 Alexis de Tocqueville studied the new nation of the United States and observed that the American obsession with material betterment and economic advancement was helping to mold a population that withdrew into isolated circles of families and friends. Mitigating this movement were voluntary organizations that brought Americans together to act in concert for the public good. Eberly and Streeter (2002) found this observation still applicable in the twenty-first century. Discussing the critical importance of the voluntary associations, the authors argue that the community-involvement roles they play at the local level help preserve the democratic way of life at the national and international levels.

The Milwaukee study found over 250 ethnic voluntary organizations in Milwaukee County. The original number from the interviews had exceeded 350, but a team of researchers refined the list to include only those with websites, telephone directory listings, or incorporation status with the state of Wisconsin, acknowledging that a possible hundred more "bedroom organizations" probably exist. Many of the functions of these ethnic organizations added value to the wider society by offering services to ethnic members and others in the wider community. These included:

- Job training
- Voter registration drives
- Services that help families adapt to change
- Leisure time activities such as festivals, parades, picnics, and dinners
- Charitable functions for ethnic members and the wider society
- Healthcare facilities

## Illuminating the Past

Tocqueville also berated Americans for forgetting their ancestors. His oft-quoted condemnation, "they clutch everything and hold nothing fast," scrutinized the tendencies of Americans to grasp material benefits wherever they could find them, form few lasting attachments, and assume that anything gained was through their own hands.

Ethnicity, by definition, is oriented toward the past, as a celebration of ancestral lineages, former homelands, passed-down traditions, and migration patterns over the centuries. Participants in the Milwaukee study were active seekers of ethnic history, often via genealogy research. Through oral histories and the examination of census records, ships' manifestos, handed-down letters, wills, birth and death records, and tax lists, they captured a history "from below." They learned about the perils and successes of their ancestors. Unwittingly, they became participants in movements to democratize history by unearthing the conditions on the ground while more powerful forces were consecrating the events that would one day appear as chapters in elementary school history texts.

But perhaps the most meaningful finding among informants studying their ancestral roots was the effect it had on their current lives. Many discussed how the knowledge of the past became transformational. By learning about tragedies, sacrifices, and accomplishments of their ancestors, they were able to put the present in perspective, assume more of a global orientation, and become much more appreciative of their current lives.

## Filling Niches

In chapter 12, informants in the Milwaukee study described the initial settlement of their families in America and Milwaukee County. The chapter also addressed the question of whether the non-Europeans made as significant a contribution to the American economy as the Europeans. Many European and non-European immigrants and migrants had actually been recruited from their former homes to work in Milwaukee County enterprises. Others arrived of their own volition and many already possessed the skills to fill a needed niche or took jobs that no one else wanted. The informants described how their immigrant or migrant generation worked long hours for low pay and made sacrifices that would improve opportunities for the next generation, and the findings were similar for the European and non-European groups. Informants from both global areas also described some of the dangerous and/or low-status jobs accepted by their earliest ethnic ancestors (sometimes very recent ones) in America, including:

- Janitorial services
- Building the transcontinental railroad
- Working in mines, foundries, and tanneries
- Hotel service
- Asbestos abatement
- Food service
- Day care work
- Domestic service
- Opening grocery stores or gas stations in disadvantaged neighborhoods
- Temp service

Other informants described skills they brought to the United States from their past home-lands, including tanning, glass blowing, metal work, printing, tool and die making, brewing, and ethnic culinary arts.

The unexpected finding in the interviews was the discussions initiated by informants on the relative work ethics of members of their ethnic groups. While informants tended to extol the work ethics of the earliest generations in the United States, this was not the case when they discussed later generations. Both the descendants of European and non-European immigrants/migrants acknowledged that jobs were much easier today than they had been in the past. However, they also suggested that the work ethic in their groups had diminished considerably over succeeding generations.

Questions remain. What factors influence the first generation to put forth the efforts they do, as reported by informants, and why is this pattern so consistent across the Milwaukee ethnic groups and times of arrival? Why do these work practices seem to wane in succeeding generations?

There are several possible explanations. One might be that the stories of struggles were embellished, either by the immigrant or migrant, or through generations of repeating the family oral histories. This might have occurred in some situations. Another explanation might be that the first generation *already* had the dispositions that made them strive before they left their former homes. Perhaps, due to temperament and early experiences, they were more likely to take risks or seek new solutions or opportunities than those who stayed behind and surrendered to hardships in their homelands. A third possible explanation is that struggle sometimes begets its own motivation. Over three quarters of the informants who had discussed the immigrant or migrant generations described immense hardships they had endured in their homelands, only to be faced with almost insurmountable challenges when they reached their destinations. Perhaps something in the struggles generated more aggression, more impetus to prove their worth, more family solidarity, and stronger ethnic support systems.

More research is needed in understanding the motivations of migrant and immigrant populations, especially as it may affect future immigration legislation. Whatever the reason for the strong work ethic and willingness to sacrifice of these first-arriving generations, the qualities were consistently manifested among both Europeans and non-Europeans.

The clear findings in the qualitative descriptions of ethnic practices in the Milwaukee study was the plethora of contributions that are being made to wider collectivities through these practices—whether the collectivity is the nation, town, neighborhood, or family. Ultimately these contributions strengthen the collectivities and help support American society.

## The Following Chapter

Chapters 14 and 15 will address the threats to ethnicity—past and present. The following chapter discusses the ideological framework that threatened ethnicity from earliest colonial times to the late twentieth century.

# Chapter Fourteen
# Life in Multi-ethnic America

Attitudes about ethnicity have evolved over the course of American history. Some of these attitudes have seriously threatened ethnicity. This chapter will discuss (a) the literature on approaches to ethnic differences, (b) stories the Milwaukee informants tell about their families' experiences in America, and (c) ways the informants compare their ethnic groups to others today.

## From the "Melting Pot" to the "Salad Bowl": The Literature on Ethnic Mixing

Over the past half century, the metaphors of the "melting pot" and, much later, the "salad bowl" have come to symbolize American expectations about ethnic adaptation. In these metaphors, ethnic cultures are likened to foods with distinctive "flavors." The foods either gradually lose their discrete pungency in a simmering pot or retain their flavors alongside complementary foods in a chilled salad bowl. The metaphor of the melting pot reigned until the late 1960s.

### The Melting Pot: The Assimilationist Approach

While the exact term "melting pot" did not come into general usage in the United States until a play of the same name was performed in 1908 in Washington, DC, the concept—as it applied to American ethnicity—had already been introduced in literature. As early as 1782, the writer Michel Guillaume Jean de Crevecoeur in *Letters from an American Farmer* claimed that all nations were melded into a "new race" of man in America (Crevecoeur, 1782). In 1845, Ralph Waldo Emerson described America as a product of a culturally and racially mixed "smelting pot" (Emerson, 1912, p. 116). And American historian Frederick Jackson Turner (1893) saw people of diverse backgrounds fusing into a "single race" in the crucible of the frontier during the westward movement.

In the twentieth century, scholars (primarily sociologists) began theorizing about the immigrant experience. The melting pot metaphor consistently nuanced their works as they attempted to explain *how* (not *if*) immigrants assimilated into American culture. Thomas and Znaniecki wrote about the disorganization and later reorganization of Polish immigrants in the United States (1984 [1918-1922]). Robert Park claimed that there was a four-step process to assimilation beginning with contact and ending with the immigrant group learning to adapt to the host culture (Park and Burgess, 1966 [1921]). Focusing on generations, Milton Gordon (1964) maintained that each succeeding generation of the immigrant family would be more like the American mainstream than their parents.

Throughout the 1950s and 1960s, social scientists writing about the immigrant experience stressed assimilation—not only as an outcome of cultural contact and acculturation—but as desired goals (Roosens, 1989). Ethnic groups would (and should) disappear into a single host society (Sandberg, 1964). Sanders (2002) described how studies aimed at showing transformations of second and later generations of ethnic groups were most often conducted by out-group members and also influenced by out-group assimilationist values. When discussing immigrants of color, these studies often harbored assumptions that they were childlike and required the assistance of the host society to manage daily lives in a modern world (Little, 1958). Inherent in the literature was one overriding point—the melting pot was never meant to be a blending of ethnicities but was intended to be all groups conforming to a relatively changeless core of old stock American identity (Banks, 1996). The broth would never pick up the flavors of the added ingredients.

## Changes in the Late 1960s

Much began to change in the 1960s. Some writers started admitting that assimilation did not work for every group (Gordon, 1964). Individuals continued to realize their potentials through membership in ethnic organizations, and ethnicity still carried weight in political arenas. Americans were not assimilating along the lines of an Anglo American prototype, as had been expected (Alba, 1990). Throughout the 1960s, African Americans, North American Indians, Latinos, and other groups began to organize for equal rights.

By late in the decade, even those scholars who had previously conducted studies on assimilation began to question whether or not the melting pot had ever accomplished its purpose. In 1970, Glazer and Moynihan wrote the watershed book, *Beyond the Melting Pot,* which questioned the metaphor's validity. They argued that ethnicity had not only endured, but might actually be gaining energy. Within the next decade many in America touted this momentum as an ethnic revival (A. D. Smith, 1981; Jacobson, 2006).

*A Reformulation*

In response to these changes in understanding ethnicity, social scientists struggled with new ways to conceptualize ethnic blending. Reflecting on the contemporary research, Eriksen (2003) claimed that the melting pot was an appropriate metaphor in the sense that diverse immigrant groups acquired the English language and often intermarried, but it did not work at other, more symbolic levels. Some scholars believed that ethnic identity itself might need rethinking. Herbert Gans (1979) introduced the term "symbolic ethnicity." Gans maintained that all US groups had been affected by acculturation and assimilation, and while ethnic bonds still held, they had radically changed. With intermarriage and loss of many ethnic neighborhoods, individuals were no longer likely to be affected by ethnicity in everyday affairs. Rather, ethnic bonds in America today might only signify nostalgic allegiance to the countries of origin, interest in ethnic history, and pride when a member of one's own group achieved something remarkable. Gans' contemporaries echoed his iteration that ethnic retention was achieved through little more than self-identification (Sanders, 2002). In this sense, ethnic groups did not lose all their flavors in a melting pot; the flavors were simply a bit less pungent than they had once been.

Other social scientists were more interested in explaining how various ethnic groups co-existed within states. As early as 1948, J. S. Furnivall developed the concept of "pluralism." The term was meant to describe ways that diverse racial and ethnic groups had been consolidated into political units. Studying social relations in Dutch and British colonies in Southeast Asia, Furnivall demonstrated how groups remained segmented with their own languages and traditions while co-existing peacefully (but with volatile undercurrents) under colonial powers (Furnivall, 1948). Furnivall saw the marketplace as the main integrating channel in these states. M. G. Smith (1984) applied the concept of pluralism to other areas of the world, particularly the Caribbean. Smith expanded the concept by de-emphasizing the marketplace and underscoring the role of the state in the peaceful, albeit inherently unstable, ethnic co-existence. He argued that without the political interference, peace would not be possible.

While some writers refined the concept of pluralism (e.g., Clarke, Ley, and Peach, 1984), others found weaknesses. Hunt and Walker (1974) applied the concept to the United States, describing how the federal government had been compelled to intervene to enforce racial integration. But these writers also found the concept problematic, because when ethnic co-existence could only exist when enforced by centralized powers, less power ended up in the hands of local groups, and the result, they argued, was anti-pluralism. Another critic (Demaine, 1984) challenged the assertion that colonialism had truly been the force behind pluralism. Others argued that the concept of pluralism and its power relations should not be limited to the internal workings of a state, but should take a world systems approach (Rex, 1986).

Eventually the concept of pluralism fell out of use, in part because of these theoretical problems, and in part because the term's meaning evolved into something denoting only a multi-ethnic population without the power relations inherent in the original Furnivall/Smith usage. What ethnic pluralism did contribute to the post-melting-pot movement was just this: Social scientists were now describing ethnic groups that mixed but did not necessarily blend.

## The Salad Bowl: The Multicultural Approach

As groups began to demand equality in resource acquisition during and after the civil rights movements, they also demanded equal influences in American cultural institutions (Burnham, 1994). Disputes were most evident in public education over curricular content, development of legislation, and other democratic processes (Kallen, 1970). Through these conflicts, a new way of conceptualizing ethnicity and inter-ethnic relations emerged, and the term "multiculturalism" came into use. Durarte and Smith define the multicultural condition and the necessary response (2000, p. 3):

> The phrase *multicultural condition* describes the demographic presence of different ethnic groups within a population along with the related factors surrounding particular groups' historical experiences, cultural beliefs, values, and social status within the society at large. By contrast, the phrase *multiculturalism* denotes a response to this condition.

Appropriate responses to the multicultural condition must include widespread knowledge of diverse cultural systems as well as acceptance and appreciation (if not celebration) of the ethnic groups' differences, similarities, and contributions. This new point of view was similar to the pluralists' ideas because a multicultural society needed some support from the state. But it also involved a good measure of voluntarism, as opposed to simple coercion, as suggested by Rex (1986, p. 164). "Those who wish to assimilate should be allowed to do so. Those who prefer to retain their separate culture should be allowed to do that. Neither a forced process of multiculturalism nor a forced process of assimilation is acceptable."

Not everyone immediately jumped on the multiculturalism bandwagon. Discussions emerged on what multiculturalism meant for individuals. Some of those in opposition took the stand that an emphasis on ethnic particularism diluted individualism in favor of collectivism, assuming this to be a negative development. Patterson (1977) claimed that the new movements put too much focus on groups and would erode any efforts toward developing a universal culture with (relatively unaffiliated) "free creative people." Hill (2000) also argued that multiculturalism (or tribalism, as he sometimes termed it) diluted individuals' opportunities to form transnational identities and rejecting, if they wished, designations of race and national identity. On the other hand, Hopper (2003) saw ethnic collectivities as leading to *more* individualism, as expressed in groups. His concerns with ethnic particularism were the proliferation of identity politics and disputes over educational curricula and public spaces.

Nevertheless, the nation moved in the direction of multiculturalism. The literature is not clear about the process through which American attitudes changed, or the extent of that change at the grassroots, but fast transformations could be observed in public education and educational curricula. Nathan Glazer in *We Are All Multiculturalists Now* (1997, p. 7) describes it well.

What is more surprising than these developments in higher education, however, is how complete has been the victory of multiculturalism in the public schools of America . . . the American public school, originally established to mold Americans of all backgrounds into a common culture and fully devoted to this task until perhaps two decades ago, has undergone a remarkable change in the last twenty years.

The melting pot concept was no longer expressed in US public education. The metaphor of the "salad bowl" gradually came to describe the new multiculturalist approach, connoting the ways various ethnic groups are juxtaposed but do not merge into a homogenous culture. The ingredients now kept their own flavors.

The next section will discuss the influences that these attitudes on ethnicity had on informants' families in the Milwaukee study.

# The Milwaukee Informants' Experiences with Ethnic Mixing

The multicultural approach to ethnic mixing did not begin to reach the general population until well into the 1990s. Because only a small number of Milwaukee informants had families that immigrated to the United States after 1990, most informants described their families' experiences as active members of ethnic groups during the melting pot phase. They recount problems they had expressing their ethnic particulars within American institutions and a population of older stock American groups.

## Anti-ethnic Policies and Practices by American Institutions

North American Indian and African American informants in the Milwaukee study described both the early and more recent problems their families faced as the result of American ethnocentric and racist policies. Examples follow.

*African American 125*: Well, of course there was slavery. My great-grandparents were slaves. You have to wonder how America would have fared without us. . . . African slavery must have accounted for a very high percentage of all the goods produced in the Americas. I wonder if the Americans would have even considered revolting against England if it had not been for the advances they'd seen under slavery. I just don't hear much about this contribution. I don't see any of my family members being thanked.

*North American Indian Creek 171*: I have letters of my ancestors from the time of Indian removal. They were Creeks who were told by the US government that they would be declared "civilized" if they had their own land and put more power in the males and held slaves. But they were still kicked off their land—even after they did all of this. But this policy of calling them civilized even kept them from other [Indian] nations when they went to Mississippi Territory. My ancestors had bought into this. You can see in their letters how much they looked down at the "wild Indians," as they called them.

*African American 190:* Redlining in housing is what I remember. We could not get loans at reasonable rates. I worked for a finance company at one time and we clearly circled high danger loans—if they lived in areas where we would not give loans.

*North American Indian Oneida 161:* My grandparents moved to Milwaukee when mom was sixteen. The reason why was [because] grandmother still feared that someone would sweep the kids away. They were still taking children away and putting them in boarding schools. . . . It used to be that if you knew the [indigenous] culture and the language you would be hurt. So if they left the reservation they wouldn't be hurt, and they already became Christians. So a lot had to do with what happened back then. The boarding school made her cold. She was beaten a lot by the Catholics.

*African American 150*: I'm not anti-busing, but in Milwaukee the tragedy was it broke up families. It ended up that families like ours had three to four kids going to three to four different schools, riding in buses for two hours. Then families could not participate in these schools, and the kids couldn't participate in extracurricular stuff. We were bused into white neighborhoods and some teachers [were] not so kindly. We got subjected to bigoted statements. . . . We didn't have kids from suburbs coming into city schools. It gave a message that there was nothing here for whites.

*North American Indian Ojibwe 169*: The Relocation Act caused my family to go into [the] city in the South. He was promised services he never got. It was a law to get Indians into the cities and not on the reservations. It was called an anti-Indian act. But you'd go to these offices in the city and sometimes there wasn't even anyone there. There was no real help.

*African American 140*: Policing practices—racial profiling. . . . I remember being followed by police when I drove through a white neighborhood—just followed for at least a mile.

*North American Indian Menomonie 160*: In 1971 or 1972 they passed the Freedom of Religion Act, finally. We used to be arrested for our beliefs. Even playing lacrosse was illegal because it was associated with "paganism."

Members of other groups at times had complex experiences with ethnic mixing. Ignatiev (2009) documents the dual nature of the Irish experience in his classic work, *How the Irish Became White*. He describes how Irish immigrants were treated as inferiors by the nativists who disparaged their Catholic faith, Democratic Party allegiance, lack of job skills, and their general support for slave power. According to Ignatiev, this experience led to political consolidation by the Irish and oppression of blacks.

> Whatever the reason, "free soil, free labor, and free men" held little appeal for the Catholic Irish population. Unable or unwilling to avail themselves of the white-skin privilege of setting themselves up as independent farmers, the vast majority clung to the Democratic Party, which continued to protect them from the nativists and guarantee them a favored position over those whom they regarded as the principal threat to their position, the free black people of the North (the only group as "free" of either property or marketable skills as the Irish). (pg. 102)

Milwaukee informants discussed other problems they had with American institutions, due in part to attitudes that Americans had about ethnicity before the 1990s.

*Mexican 184*: My grandmother is actually from an area in Texas which used to be a part of Mexico. It got divided. Some of my family lived in the US—in Texas and California—all around the border. And some of my family was in Mexico. When the southwest was annexed by the United States, it resulted in Mexico losing one third of its territory. Then after Mexico was divided, the immigration laws weren't like we know them now. There were times when the US needed Mexican labor. They would lessen the laws to allow Mexicans to come [and] work. But when the economy is bad, immigrants are treated like criminals.

*Jewish 124*: Institutions of higher learning had quotas for Jewish enrollment. There would only be so many numbers in places like Columbia and Yale. This was not illegal then.

*Scots Irish 181*: My great grandfather was Chinese. My great grandmother was Scots Irish and he ended up with her because the government had passed an immigration law that said he could not bring his family from China over here. And in Washington he could not marry a white person either. So he was stuck here without any money and ended up with my grandmother, although they never got legally married.

US policy and corresponding public opinion often came down hard on some ethnic groups because of war. Sometimes these policies resulted in some individuals trying to deny their heritage, if they were able to pass.

*Italian 122*: But you do understand when World War II came and Italy was on the side of the Axis so to speak, and they lost their boats? Joe DiMaggio's father was a fisherman. He [the son] was a very famous ball player. Anyway, his father lost his boat. After the war of course they got them back. . . . You read about how the Japanese were interned. They did that to the Italians too. The funny thing was there was a man, they took his boat away from him because he was Italian, probably wasn't a citizen yet, but then no one knew how to run the boat, so they hired him back to run the boat.

*German 179*: It was difficult at the time of the First World War and people we knew who were Schmidts became Smiths. And there was always that anti-German difficulty but in Milwaukee you know the German-speaking population and the descendents of German speakers through the years have had a majority basically, so it wasn't quite as bad as in some other areas.

*English 181*: Many people think that the English never suffered persecution in this country, because being English was almost the norm here. But few know that after the Revolutionary War, many of those that sided with the English (and were English) lost their lands. My ancestor was a British Indian trader and because the English were more lenient in their policies toward the Natives, most traders sided with the English in the War. But because of this, a large group of Indian traders, including my ancestors, had their lands confiscated after the Americans won the war, even though they had been in America for over one hundred years at the time.

*French 138*: We always faced accusations of being collaborators with the Germans during World War II and not backing some American international policies. I rarely go to a cocktail party where someone knows I'm French where I don't have to respond to some remarks like, "Hey we rescued your asses in World War II and World War I and where are you when we need help?"

## Anti-ethnic Attitudes at the Grassroots

Many of the Milwaukee informants discussed problems that their families faced from other Americans, because of their ethnic identities and practices.

*Kashubian 193*: People from all over Milwaukee looked down on us. Jones Island [a peninsula within Milwaukee County where the Kashubes organized a fishing village] was called a menagerie. There was a boat captain that took people on cruises and they would pass the island and talk about us. "Look, see, there's people that live there." We were an attraction. Even today you will see an old Pole referring to someone as a Kashube if that person is thought to be low class.

*Irish 127*: When we started to come over in big numbers, especially after the famine, we were considered anathema. They said we were a different race of people and you'd see these signs put up by employers, "No Irish Need Apply." People said we were dirty and dangerous.

*Russian 161*: You have to understand, when I was growing up, that we were told, you know, never to tell anyone that we were Russian—that we had any kind of Russian heritage. And you know, that was actually worse than to say that we were Jewish, or ethnically Jewish. My parents converted when I was seven, but Russians were, you know, horribly evil, akin to how people feel [today] about some of the Middle Eastern countries. So that was nothing that we could ever discuss or really explore in public.

*African American 112*: Neighborhoods would organize to keep us out. I remember once seeing a sign that said, "If they move in, your neighbors will move out." I was maybe about twelve at the time and I wondered what was so—eek—about us that no one wanted to be near us.

Another issue was stereotypes, or unreliable generalizations about members of a group that do not take individual differences into account (Schaefer, 2007). Informants discussed the rumors and stereotypes they often encountered from more assimilated, but not necessarily knowledgeable, Milwaukeeans.

*Polish 153*: We were considered stupid, like "How many Polacks does it take to screw in a light bulb?" kind of thing. The other thing was that people said they heard we were dirty, when we probably kept the cleanest properties in the city.

*Venezuelan 120*: I take as an insult when someone comes in here and says, "Oh, it's so clean." They don't realize why they're saying that, but it goes back to paradigm. They think we all live in trees in the jungle.

*Slovenian 195*: I hate the word "slovenly." Mostly I find it funny and sometimes frustrating that no one seems to know where Slovenia is.

*African Somali 161*: Well yeah they assume that everybody grew up around, you know, elephants. But most of us saw our first elephants at the zoo here in Milwaukee.

*Palestinian 132*: [The first is the] terrorist thing, which, if you look back in history is more western nations that started terrorism. I think people don't take the time to realize [that] there is individual [sic] sponsored terrorism, and state sponsored terrorism. They don't take the time to find that there are individuals who act out that don't represent the community, they don't represent the nation. . . . I don't think any of those people in prison or Oklahoma City is representative of the American people or Christians—or that David Koresh is representative of Christians. I think people need to take the time to really think about things and not rush to judgments and accept these blanket statements.

*Japanese 111*: In school, I noticed that Americans think that we are all good with math and science. I suck at chemistry. Also, Americans, or Western men somehow believe that Japanese girls are like ultra-submissive. There always are some Western guys with "submissive Asian girl" fantasy coming to Japan to get married, but after they get married, they find out that girls are not as submissive as they thought, and they get into domestic violence.

*German 121*: The Nazi thing. Most people don't realize that probably 90 to 99 percent of the Germans that are here in the United States came here before the word Nazi was invented. But you see this in TV shows with the person with the German accent always being portrayed as militaristic and a slave to order, like the Nazi image.

*Indian 171*: I should say they have the impression like from the movie *Slumdog Millionaire*. Have you seen that? They think India is all slums, that the culture is all orthodox, that we are all having arranged marriages. But that's not the thing. They should come and see India and they can definitely change their minds and understand better.

*African Guinea Malinke 140*: Many people in America tend to think that in Africa, you know, all of them live in the jungle, which is not true. It is a misrepresentation of the African society. Some, you know, are from villages, some, you know, are from the city—grew up in the city. They have a lot [of] Western influences in their life [sic] even though [they] strongly believe in African traditions.

*Filipino 130*: When the Americans came to the Philippines in 1898 they referred to the natives as monkeys. It's no secret—it's part of American history. We were taken aback by that. . . . People don't even know where the Philippines are.

*Scottish 150*: I bristle at the aspect of people trying to portray the Scots as some sort of burly, red-haired, sort of unkempt caricatures who are just sort of foul mouthed and brusque and ready to pick a fight at any time.

*Black Muslim 146*: Muslim women are portrayed as subservient and without a voice. Muslim women were the first to receive liberation, have the right to own property, have control of their own money, and marry whom they please.

*Italian 130*: Italians are represented in many movies as being part of the mafia. *The Godfather, Goodfellas, The Sopranos.*

*Hmong 142*: People always accuse us if there is a cat missing or anything—that we'd caught it and eaten it. They say we are backwards, and we are—or were.

*North American Indian Ojibwe 167*: Lot of misrepresentation in stereotyping. People portray us how we were one hundred years ago.

*Jewish 104*: In my childhood a common expression was "He will Jew you out of something." That meant that he was going to cheat, swindle you out of something. That expression is not used that much anymore, but the idea is still there. My mother used to say that Jews tip more in restaurants just to overcome the stingy stereotype. I know that Jews give a large amount to charities.

*African American 119*: They put us all into one or two categories—we're lazy or all entertainers.

*German Russian 175*: There were times in the Dakotas in which the people who were not German Russians were very prejudiced against us because we tended to live in places, in sod houses and that. So they considered us to be very dirty people (even though we were very immaculate) because we had mud houses and everything. So, there was prejudice against us.

*Puerto Rican 144*: Puerto Ricans have been portrayed as drug addicts, people who carry knives. The media has influenced a lot of that.

*African Nigerian Ibo 105*: They talk like we are backwards. They don't know that when Europe was in the Middle Ages, we had strong African kingdoms—much richer than what was in Europe. We Ibos are very well educated, and most people think everyone in Africa is some kind of a hunter gatherer.

*Mexican 165:* When you look at television, they are always portrayed as gangsters or migrant workers. It's a bad portrayal. Because if you only see someone in a certain role, you begin to believe and expect them to be only able to do certain things.

*Irish 134*: [They said] we kept pigs in our bedrooms. We were part of a conspiracy to make the Pope king of the world.

*Scots Irish 108*: I don't think people talk about the Scots Irish at all in town. I think that's the bigger issue—especially when you consider how very much we contributed to this country.

## Recent Changes

For some Milwaukeeans, assertions that positive changes in ethnic tolerance have taken place might seem absurd considering what happened in 2012, at the very end of the Milwaukee study. On August 5, 2012, a white supremacist gunman stormed a Sikh temple in the Milwaukee County village of Oak

Creek, shooting six people and wounding four others. However, the response by Milwaukeeans (and indeed people all over the world) was revealing. Grassroots groups in Milwaukee neighborhoods, organizations, and churches immediately organized to hold candlelight vigils in support of the Sikh community. President Obama ordered flags at all US federal buildings to be flown at half staff. Political leaders, callers to radio talk shows, news anchors, and bloggers condemned ethnic and racial intolerance for months after the episode. When protests against the US arose in India, many Milwaukee Sikhs condemned the actions. A man interviewed by a reporter on a Milwaukee street declared: "This is the twenty-first century, not the Middle Ages or Jim Crow. How can this hatred happen?"

The reactions to this massacre suggest that ethnic and racial tolerance is gaining strength in the county. Some of the informants in the Milwaukee study discussed additional ways attitudes have changed over ethnic differences in recent years. To some, the change is real; to others, sincerity is still lacking.

*Mexican 119*: There used to be these jokes about the Mexicans like the jokes about the Poles. That has mainly changed. Today with the ethnic festivals and things, I think people have changed.

*Belgian Flemish 109*: Maybe people have stopped their jokes, but I would love to see a single person who knows what I'm talking about when I say I'm Flemish. I don't know that they teach anything about the cultures in the schools in the US, or if they do, maybe just a few groups.

*North American Indian Cherokee 184*: Things are a little better. I think there's a sort of political correctness around and you don't hear the really bad slurs on Indians. But at the same time I don't get the feeling that people know any more about us.

*French 191*: It's improved, for sure. For a long time Canada had this mosaic idea about cultures, while we still wanted everyone to assimilate. It's catching on here.

*Kashubian 133*: Ha, ha. Today there're people wanting to find out all about us, now that we've assimilated so much. Even some of the Poles accept us—some not so much.

*African American 148*: I don't know if much has changed. You see the more educated people being careful with what they say. I still see the same prejudice, to be honest. I don't see people asking a whole lot of questions about us.

*German 152*: I think so much damage has already been done. I don't see much pride left among the Germans I know.

With the negative experiences the Milwaukee informants described in the United States, one might wonder what their attitudes are about these same Americans. The next section discusses ways that the Milwaukee informants talk about others.

# The Milwaukee Informants' Discussions of Other Ethnic Groups

In the preceding section, Milwaukee informants discussed their families' experiences with inter-ethnic mixing and the stereotypes they heard about their own groups. These reports are consistent with the bias against ethnic particularism that pervaded the country before the multiculturalist perspective began to take hold. The bias existed in government policies (more on this will be discussed in the following chapter) and in the attitudes of the general population— individuals not necessarily deeply involved in their own ethnic groups. But now we fast-forward to the present and listen to individuals who are deeply involved in their ethnic groups. The semi-structured questionnaire posed a series of questions that encouraged informants to discuss other ethnic groups and compare their own groups to the others.

## Describing Similarities among Groups

Milwaukee informants rarely expressed ethnocentric sentiments. Throughout the interviews remarks extolled the virtues of multiculturalism. For example, when asked what they liked about Milwaukee, the second most frequently coded response (after size of the area) was ethnic diversity. The informants also tended to find more similarities than differences between their ethnic group and others.

More than any population in the Milwaukee sample, the North American Indians consistently found similarities between their own beliefs and practices and those of other groups. Even when they were asked about appropriate and inappropriate borrowing of their traditions by other groups, they often found ways to turn the subject back to similar practices.

*North American Indian Oneida 121*: There are a lot of tribal heritage cultures like African Americans and Mexicans, and they have the same value system as Indians. Africans say it takes a whole village to raise a child. This is integral to Indian communities—every Indian family believes that. There are so many similarities.

*North American Indian Oneida 181*: I see similarities between other groups— not so much borrowed. The Polish have family closeness, and the extended family values like us.

*North American Indian Stockbridge Munsee 153*: African churches are similar in some ways, with drumming.

*North American Indian Ojibwe 154*: It isn't so much borrowing—there is much [that] a lot of groups have in common, such as smoke used as purification in many cultures. We find a lot of similarities in black and Hispanic culture—lots of laid-back people, and the respect for elders.

*North American Indian Potawatomie 190*: One group that parallels with us is Asian, especially the Hmong, because they have a lot of the same philosophies that we have. The healing and respect for elders and ancestors. A lot of things they do are so much the same. We include many Mexicans as Indians, but we closely identify with Asian culture because of similarities.

Members of other groups also tended to find more similarities than differences. Of the responses that were coded "ethnic comparisons," similarities were over three times more prevalent than differences. Their remarks also suggest that the informants made efforts to learn about other groups.

*Slovenian 155*: Poles and Slovenians seem to have a similar temperament and history. . . . A Slovenian wedding and a Polish wedding were almost the same growing up in Milwaukee. The blood sausage that Poles call *kiszka* is the same as the Slovenian sausage by a different name. We always called it by its Polish name. Both nationalities like sausages of all kinds. They shared working class neighborhoods and hobbies like bowling. My nephews all bowled with their parents although they are now one-quarter Slovenian. Probably my favorite instance of Poles and Slovenians sharing a tradition is the blessing of the baskets on Holy Saturday before Easter.

*Norwegian 143*: I think the Hispanics in Milwaukee with all their festivals and parades—they're pretty much similar to Norwegians—you know, with the flag flying. And they got their day, *Cinco de Mayo* [as Norwegians have May 17, *Syttende Mai*].

*German 120*: In Milwaukee, we were probably the most tolerant of African Americans. There's lots of similarities in practices—the love of the family tavern, music, other leisure time activities. They moved into our neighborhoods while the Poles and other groups kept them out. Germans in America had a long history of opposing slavery.

*Polish 111*: The Mexicans would move into our neighborhoods in all of the cities. We were both Catholic, kept grandma in the home, took our kids to dances, and played polkas.

*Hmong 152*: Somalis are like us and other Africans generally—with the bride price and all.

*African American 105*: Because we were not able to own land in many states, we kind of settled in cities where we could get other kind of work. In some es the businesses brought us up from the South to work in their factories. We were sort of like the Jews in that they couldn't own land too in European areas and found jobs in the cities early on.

*Hmong 112:* The Mexican and the Hmong seem to be most alike. People really depend on each other to help out.

*Mexican 101:* Poles always took their kids to the dances. We take our kids to the dances also.

*Irish 105:* Italians took unskilled spots on railroads and then learned the skills and they were also Catholic. I think we're a lot like them.

## Describing Differences among Groups

While the informants did not describe differences nearly as often as they described similarities, even when they did, they usually described the differences in positive or non-judgmental ways.

*African American 143:* When we are in the church, we are *really* in the church. . . . Our services last until they are done. We don't keep set times like the Europeans. We get into it and the preacher can preach as long as it suits him or the choir can sing as long as they want.

*English 135:* I think we have been pretty individualistic, at least since perhaps the Enlightenment. I see other cultures that are less so—perhaps more lineage or community minded—like the Irish and many Latino groups. Most of the Asians too.

*Greek 183:* Greeks love music, dancing, food, celebrate name days. We show our feelings on our sleeves. We're not as stoic as the Irish, Germans, English.

*North American Indian Oneida 194:* It's different in the city. The kids were raised on the rez to not draw attention to themselves. But teachers see this as inattentiveness. Our kids learn differently. . . . This makes us different from other cultures like Jewish and African American and perhaps Greeks and Italians. I think that the families [in the other groups] urge their kids to be a bit more aggressive, not just stand in the background.

*Mexican 175:* I had culture shock. I came from a country where you always had to respect the authority, never to question them. And another thing—the hardest part—I am used to touching, hugging people. It is hard for people to understand. They will push me away. So I would go home and cry on my bed, because this European I want to hug only pushes me away. I didn't realize that some people not of my background need their personal space. It was one of the hardest things for me to learn.

In addition, Latino informants of diverse national origins often made points of differentiating themselves from Latinos from other origins.

> *Puerto Rican 104*: We don't mix music at all. Unless there is an intermarried couple, such as a Mexican and a Puerto Rican, the music doesn't mix. There is Salsa and [Dominican] Meringue for Puerto Ricans, which is very different from traditional Mexican music. . . . If you consider South American music, the style is completely different. Cuban, Dominican, and Puerto Rican music, all being from the Caribbean, are closely related in terms of the beats and the themes of the music.

> *Mexican 192*: People often think Mexicans in Milwaukee are just like Puerto Ricans. This is not the case at all. For one thing, you see most Mexicans on the south side and most Puerto Ricans on the north side. There are so many differences in food and music and dance and even family types, but also Mexicans tended to be Spaniards mixed with the indigenous population and Puerto Ricans were often Spaniards and other Europeans mixed with Africans. You see a lot of African customs in the Caribbean which were not picked up in Mexico, especially in the Catholic religion.

> *Bolivian 185*: It's about the music. You see differences in the music. We have this little guitar called the *charango*. It has twelve strings. And they have a flute called the *sampona*. It's like a flute. . . . Some of its influence from the Spanish and the rest is from the Inca.

> *Chilean 155*: I'm from South America, and I don't like to put Latinos in one bag. I think we're very different—I don't eat tortillas and beans. . . . I lived in Mexico for awhile and between the lighter skins and the darker skins, there's a lot of tension. In Chile, you won't find a lot of racial differences, but you'll find a lot of class differences. Mexicans are more conservative and religious. And Chileans aren't so religious.

## Expressing Negative Opinions

Throughout over six thousand pages of interview transcripts, very few examples emerged of the Milwaukee informants expressing negative opinions of other ethnic groups—not even among informants representing groups in conflict on the international stage, such as the Middle East. When it did happen, it was nearly always under two circumstances: (1) when the informant was raised in another country, and (2) when an informant believed that members of another ethnic group in close proximity were directly impinging on the informant's quality of life.

*Raised in Another Country*

While most nations have undergone some evolution in attitudes about ethnic differences, the movement from the melting pot to the salad bowl was primarily a US phenomenon. In the Milwaukee project, some informants who were raised abroad had not been enculturated in ethnic tolerance—and much less, in celebration. Their remarks about other ethnic groups sometimes reflected this difference in background.

> *African Ibo 142*: I think a lot of Africans look down at African Americans. We want to know: Why can't they get an education, get ahead? Why do they get handouts?

> *Serbian 191*: These blacks [shakes head]. Uncivilized. See how they act on TV with all the screaming [during the Hurricane Katrina crisis]? Who did this Martin Luther King think he was?

> *Mexican 144*: I don't like it when they call me a Mexican. I came from Mexico but my family absolutely never mixed with the indigenous people. We have family records as proof. We are whites. It's just because we came from Mexico that we are branded Mexican.

*Living in Multi-cultural Neighborhoods*

Anthropologists in the Milwaukee study recruited a representative sample (approximately half) of all informants from multi-ethnic, often transitioning, neighborhoods. The purpose was to compare informants' attitudes of other ethnic groups by the types of neighborhoods they lived in. Those informants living in neighborhoods known for ethnic and racial diversity tended to express some of the most positive remarks about their diverse neighbors, but tended to express some of the most negative remarks as well.

*Example 1.* The "MP" neighborhood had once been an Irish stronghold. For the past several decades, African Americans moved in, and currently are the majority in MP. Both Irish and African Americans were interviewed.

> *Irish 181*: I am so glad I raised my child here. I remember the first black family here. They went to [name of Catholic church]. She asked to pick up my son, who was just a baby, and I cringed, as I'd never known a black person before. But I let her. And that started so many friendships. I have to say now that I just love their giving attitude. Whenever I have a problem and need help, I nearly always go to one of my black friends before one of my white ones.
> *Irish 150*: Sometimes I can't take them [African Americans]. The loudness. The screaming at their kids.

> *African American 149*: I got so much help from the Irish in MP. [Name of a politician] got me a great contact with the city. They know how to work it [politics], while we're just learning.

*African American 191*: The Irish tried to keep us out when we started coming here. Why are they still in power in the neighborhood, I'd like to know. There's so many more of us.

*Example 2.* "HM" is a neighborhood that had been predominantly Polish until the 1960s, when Latinos—primarily of Mexican descent—began to move in.

*Polish 120*: I love nearly all my Hispanic neighbors. They are the best parents. . . . To be honest, I almost wish I'd had them as role models when my kids were young.

*Polish 125*: When this was a Polish neighborhood you never saw this litter. These Mexicans can't keep their property up. We used to wash the sidewalks every week.

*Mexican 119*: I loved what they [Polish] did with this neighborhood. I love the businesses they developed that are still around. I love the way they built the sturdy homes.

*Mexican 116*: When we first came here, the gangs were not Latino—[they] were Polish. . . . Poles had a lot of ethnic organizations and there were a lot of white kids in the gangs. It was hard to get beyond [Name] Avenue because they had their own groups, their own gangs.

*Example 3.* "SP" is a neighborhood that since the 1970s has attracted middle-class African Americans and European Americans—mostly Germans and Czechs. In the 1990s a large community of Chasidic Jews began to move into SP.

*African American 103*: I met my [Jewish] husband here, but he wasn't Orthodox. He's taught me so much of the culture and, I must say, I'm enthralled.

*African American 126*: We were here before them [Chasidic Jews], but since they came, we have lost our neighborliness. They don't invite us to their homes. Their kids don't play with ours. When we have a neighborhood event, they all sit together at one table and don't mix.

*German 166*: This new Jewish element—I think it's increased our property values. I feel a sense of calm when I see them walking to the synagogue on Saturday mornings. I think all their cultural characteristics are fascinating—their dress, their holidays, their music. On the other hand, they haven't shown much interest in our older neighbors here, and there have been some complaints.

*Jewish 110*: I was surprised to see how much we had in common. When we oppose some new development in our neighborhood, they [African Americans] see the same problems.

*Jewish 112*: The black population is largely responsible for committing a lot of the crimes that are going on in the neighborhood. I don't know that whites are specifically targeted as victims of the crimes. I think that people that want to steal, a lot of them would do it no matter who the property belonged to. On one hand, there is a racial correlation to the increase in crime. On the other hand I don't think it can be attributed to racial hostility.

The following example from field notes shows how a Milwaukee neighborhood found ways to celebrate its diversity.

*Field Notes: April, 2012*
"LV" is home to a mélange of ethnic businesses serving its primarily Latin American, Eastern European, and American Indian populations. One can walk into a bakery on LV's main street and be greeted in Spanish, and walk a few doors down to a deli and be addressed in Polish. These businesses are scattered throughout the neighborhood, mirroring the balanced layout of LV's diverse populations. Other physical markers of ethnic collaboration in LV include two ceramic art pillars situated in the neighborhood's central park. Created in 2009 and 2011 by youth from area schools, the pillars display imagery celebrating the accomplishments of LV's major ethnic groups. The first showcases Mexican, Polish, and American Indian history; the second features the history of German, Puerto Rican, and African American residents.

Today, representatives of the three largest ethnic groups, Mexican, Polish, and American Indian, are having their last meeting to plan the tri-cultural celebration for the first weekend in May, coinciding with *Cinco de Mayo*, Polish Independence Day, and the birthday of an Ojibwe community leader. The organizers hammer out the details of flyer distribution, the schedule for picking up food from local restaurants, and the final number of ethnic organizations that have committed to participate. The event will include a parade, ethnic food, and tents to showcase identities, traditions, and shared values.

# Implications for Larger Collectivities: Ethnic Involvement and Tolerance of Diversity

Evolving attitudes about ethnic particularism in the United States, which were reflected in (and perhaps influenced by) the social science literature of the times, most likely affected the often difficult experiences that the Milwaukee informants discussed with American policy and the general public. On the other hand, when the informants today discuss other ethnic groups in the United States, most of their comments show knowledge of other ethnic groups' cultures and histories, and tolerance (sometimes celebration) of other groups' cultures. Negative comments were rare, and were made mostly by recent immigrants whose countries of origin may not have experienced the widespread changes in attitudes about diversity that the United States had. Others who sometimes expressed negative opinions lived in close proximity to other ethnic groups where neighborhood conflicts tended to emerge. Getting along often came down to questions such as: Did the groups support each other's agenda? Were some groups perceived as contributing to social disorganization? Did some appear less courteous and neighborly?

However, even among informants living in close proximity to other groups, positive comments occurred more frequently than negative ones. A question arises: Are individuals who are *deeply involved in their own ethnic practices* likely to be more tolerant, even appreciative, of other ethnic groups? A national survey has suggested that, like the European Americans, African Americans, Latinos, and Asian Americans also held stereotypical views of other racial and ethnic groups. For example, nearly half of the African Americans surveyed agreed that Asian Americans were "crafty and devious" in business (National Conference of Christians and Jews, 1994). The survey did not indicate the extent that the respondents were involved in their own ethnic groups. Some circumstances have been shown to diminish intolerance. Schaefer (2007) describes studies in chapter 2 of *Race and Ethnicity in the United States* that suggest that prejudice can be reduced, at least temporarily, by formal education, equal treatment of ethnic and racial groups in the mass media, equal-status contact, and diversity training in the workplace. Might strong participation in one's own ethnic practices be another influence? A limited amount of educational research is available that suggests that youth with strong ethnic pride are more likely to be appreciative of other groups (Gonzales and Cause, 1995; Vinson and Neimeyer, 2000), but few rigorous studies of ethnic adults on this topic have been conducted. The Milwaukee informants repeatedly expressed favorable opinions of other ethnic groups, as well as general knowledge of their cultures and histories. Was this simply because they were interviewed during the multiculturalist period, or was this an outgrowth of the informants' profound involvement in their own US ethnic groups? The quotes presented throughout this book suggest the latter, but a descriptive qualitative study without a control group cannot answer this question definitively. Clearly more research is needed in this direction.

## The Following Chapter

Life in multi-cultural America had been threatened by schools of thought on assimilation and cohabitation since colonial times. Chapter 15 will discuss ways that ethnicity has been threatened since the middle of the twentieth century.

# Chapter Fifteen
# Threats to Ethnicity

Chapter 14 summarized the difficulties that ethnic groups experienced living in a society where they often faced cultural pressures to assimilate to an Anglo-American ideal. This chapter will discuss pressures these groups confront more often in recent times, including twentieth-century urban policies that broke up ethnic neighborhoods and current trends in American culture that can inhibit the transmission of ethnic ways.

## Effects of Urban Policies on Ethnic Neighborhoods

From the middle to late twentieth century, urban policies were often a major threat to ethnicity. During the decades when melting pot ideals reigned, it was common for scholars to measure an ethnic group's assimilation by the rates in which they left ethnic enclaves—most often those in urban neighborhoods (e.g., Duncan and Duncan, 1955; Duncan and Lieberson, 1959; Lieberson, 1963). The assumption was that families who moved away from their fellow ethnics would gradually abandon their ethnic practices. While this loss of proximity changed ethnicity to a more voluntary involvement, it also sometimes weakened ethnic ties (Alba, 1990). The developments that most impacted ethnic neighborhoods were urban renewal and expressway building.

### Federal Legislation

Two federal acts played key roles in urban renewal and expressway building. The first of these was the American Housing Act of 1949, which included an extensive expansion of the federal role in public housing and provided financing for slum clearance programs associated with urban renewal efforts across the United States. Between 1953 and 1986, the federal government spent $13.5 billion on urban redevelopment and slum clearance projects, reshaping the landscape of American cities during the post-war era.

The second piece of legislation was the Federal-Aid Highway Act of 1956, also known as the National Interstate and Defense Highways Act (Teaford, 1990). The money for the act was administered through a highway trust fund where the federal government would pay 90 percent of construction costs and the states would pay 10 percent. Ultimately the interstate system comprised nearly forty-seven thousand miles at a total cost of nearly $129 billion. The focus of the program was moving traffic in and out of central cities as expeditiously as possible. As in the case of urban renewal, areas considered slums were targeted for razing.

## Results of the Policy across the Country

Urban renewal and expressway construction fractured ethnic neighborhoods across the United States. Pointing to examples in Chicago, Philadelphia, Detroit, and Boston, Jones (2004) claimed that Protestant "ruling elites" used urban renewal policies and projects to move mainly Catholic ethnic groups from the cities to the suburbs between 1930 and the late 1980s. Other writers focused on the removal of ethnic groups that were not necessarily Catholic. The combination of urban renewal programs and highway construction cost Baltimore most of the Franklin-Mulberry Corridor, where 89 percent of the displaced community was African American (Gioielle, 2011). In Miami, the Overton neighborhood—also known by locals as "the Harlem of the South"—lost 148 businesses and up to forty thousand African American and Caribbean residents, due to freeway construction and urban renewal (Dluhy, Revell, and Wong, 2002). In Boston, urban renewal razed the Italian and Jewish neighborhoods of the West End (Gans, 1999). African Americans again were displaced in the St. John neighborhood in Flint, Michigan, through an urban renewal project (Highsmith, 2009). Urban renewal resulted in the removal of both African American and immigrant Jewish communities in Washington, DC (Lavine, 2012). In Cleveland, African Americans in three neighborhoods were displaced by urban renewal (Jenkins, 2001).These are just a few of the examples nationwide.

In most cases cited in the literature, the decisions on neighborhoods to be razed for either highway construction or urban renewal were made by coalitions of government officials, business leaders, and (occasionally) citizen groups. "Blight" was the operative word used to justify areas to be razed, referring to deterioration and decay of buildings due to neglect, crime, or lack of economic support. Very often, the neighborhoods selected for redevelopment were those close to downtown commercial centers. Civic leaders often argued that these areas could be better used for projects such as highways that would move people in and out of the center of the city or for downtown revitalization projects. The ethnic neighborhoods that were razed were often self-contained communities, with their own business districts, faith communities, schools, community centers, and ethnic institutions (Aponte-Pares, 2000). However, both major expressway construction and urban renewal projects took place during decades when the melting pot ideology reigned and preserving ethnic practices was not a priority.

The above-mentioned rationales also applied to highway building and urban renewal in Milwaukee.

## The Milwaukee Examples

Milwaukee lost a number of ethnic neighborhoods between 1950 and 1980 due to urban renewal, expressway building, and the combination of both. Included in the losses were the predominantly African American Bronzeville neighborhood just north of downtown, "Little Italy" in the Third Ward just south of downtown, the heavily Irish/Czech Tory Hill neighborhood in the northern section of downtown, and "Little Puerto Rico" in the eastern section of downtown (Jansen, 1999; Sanders, 2000; Tolan, 2003). Other ethnic neighborhoods that were not completely razed, but lost significant housing, were Milwaukee's southside *Polonia*, and the heavily Irish Merrill Park on the city's west side.

Milwaukee informants discussed the long-term effects of the loss of these neighborhoods, including what it did to community and commercial life.

*African American 131*: The loss of Bronzeville was the breakdown of the village. The whites had people moving them into the projects and those with a little money moved to the suburbs. It was then the image of who we were that came from the whites. Before that it had been a localized culture. Before that you took care of your own—you watched other people's kids, made sure your neighborhood was nice and safe. After the move, we lost that.

*African American 110*: Do you have any idea how many businesses we had along Walnut Street and on either side? Look into the *Negro Yellow Pages* in 1950. Hundreds. These were businesses that had been passed on from parents to children. And what happened to them? Well, some tried to reopen in those other neighborhoods, but the whites never came. If you wonder why there aren't that many black businesses today in Milwaukee, well, here's your answer.

*African American 180*: Before you had well-meaning people [that] sold homes to blacks whose rent was going toward the price of the house. But after urban renewal and the expressway, the blacks ended up with nothing then, because the money was paid to the homeowners and did not go to them.

*Italian 192*: I remember I was a little kid and you weren't against it [urban renewal], but it was the first urban renewal project the city undertook, and they were well intentioned, but they didn't realize the devastation it brought to the community.

*Italian 128*: So many food businesses were lost, never to return. Friends and families were split up.

*Italian 123*: There was our church, what people called "the little pink church." It was the center of our community. It brought us together. Everyone knew that's where you got married, had your kids baptized, met up with your friends. With the loss of our homes came the loss of this center as well.

*Puerto Rican 111*: We used to live in a downtown neighborhood, about where [name of downtown neighborhood] was. Our church was [name] and we did well there. We had some stores, lots of extended families. Then the City decided to move us out because some of our homes were old. They were old when we moved there. Homes get old. They didn't give us money to fix them up. We were just told to move. In came urban renewal and later the freeway. Most of us never got any funds to relocate or anything.

*Polish 150*: The expressway was built in the 1950s and 1960s and it took a lot of homes. It took older homes. They [the Poles] wanted to stay but there were no homes available. When some had to leave then others followed.

*Polish 176*: The expressway cut the [name of church] community in two. They were one community and then they were two.

*Irish 185*: The freeway broke our neighborhood in two. It took out so much housing, some of it very nice housing. Some Irish had to move away. People were convinced this would be a good thing, that people could get on that freeway and go anywhere. The truth is that now we just have people driving *through* our neighborhood to get on or off the freeway. They don't stop and use our businesses.

*Irish 169*: The Irish have left the old neighborhoods. They dispersed and continue to disperse. But we haven't lost our pride in ethnicity. We still have family. We have dancing and pubs and restaurants and festivals. We have Irish Fest and St. Patrick's Day and we still get together for that.

And what happened to these communities? The Irish scattered throughout Milwaukee and the city's suburbs, and eventually developed an Irish community center in the 1990s directly between their two former neighborhoods. Some Puerto Ricans resettled on the eastern boundaries of a Milwaukee central city neighborhood called Riverwest, and many others migrated to the city's South Side. The Italians scattered throughout Milwaukee and its suburbs, but in the 1990s made the decision to erect an Italian community center in their old neighborhood in the Third Ward. Many of the Poles remained in their old southside *Polonia*, while others continued migrating to Milwaukee's southern suburbs, where they ultimately established a community center. African Americans were even more greatly affected by the loss of Bronzeville. Many of the lower income blacks remained in the central city where they could access public housing, while others scattered north and northwest, and later, to the South Side. They had lost their center. Like the

Italians and the Irish, they recently began a campaign to recreate the center—a new Bronzeville. See field notes below.

*Field Notes: February, 2012*
The line was nearly a block long. Most of the people waiting would not be able to enter the carnival-sized tent behind the building they came to tour. Most would not see the mayor of Milwaukee cutting the ribbon or hear the black historians talking about the history of this building in old Bronzeville.

The ceremony was organized to welcome back an historic building that had gone through several incarnations (as a library, youth club, and art council) in the old neighborhood. The building was now to become a major community center at the southern tip of the *new* Bronzeville. When the City of Milwaukee responded to African American demands to rebuild the hub of the black community, the Common Council agreed to set aside an area for development of a new Bronzeville—not bordering downtown as it once had, but anchored about a mile north of the old neighborhood. With this decision, the African American community was inviting and gradually adding black developments to the area. Tonight it was the community center, and a very animated crowd pressed forward.

Across the country, the loss of the ethnic neighborhoods to urban renewal and freeway building may have dispersed the groups but did not completely annihilate them. In Milwaukee, the ethnics reorganized and found new centers. But other influences in American culture were having subtle but profound effects on ethnic reproduction.

# Contemporary Trends in American Culture

Until very late in the twentieth century, US ethnic groups experienced pressures to assimilate to Anglo-American ideals. While some Milwaukee informants still felt those pressures, most discussed the process of becoming "Americanized" in different contexts. To these informants, Americanization involved practices aimed at socioeconomic mobility or contemporary child-rearing ideals.

## Americanization and Socioeconomic Mobility

Ideas on the so-called American dream have changed over the past decades. JWK, a marketing communications firm, conducted a survey of over five hundred US adults over eighteen in 2012 and found that the linchpins of the American dream in this sample have changed from religious faith, family, and community to winning recognition and making and spending money (Smith, 2012). The latter interpretation of the American dream has long permeated ethnic literature on the socioeconomic mobility of American ethnic groups (e.g., Farley and Alba, 2002; Glazer and Moynihan, 1970; Gold, 2006; Zhou, 1997). The assumption in most texts is that attaining higher education, purchasing homes in highly regarded neighborhoods (ideally suburban), achieving high-status occupations, and increasing material wealth were signs that an ethnic group had captured the American dream. In the Milwaukee study, many informants indicated they were seeking upward mobility through education and employment. However, many also saw drawbacks—particularly when jobs and careers were all-consuming and might require moving away from families and the ethnic community. While substantial differences in opinions or actions by age or gender rarely emerged among Milwaukee informants when they discussed ethnic practices, this was not the case when discussing Americanization. Most of the informants that expressed concerns about the drawbacks of upward mobility were females under the age of fifty-five.

*Chinese 175*: I think nowadays with the jobs that families realize that the children have to go elsewhere for jobs and work, and that has assisted the thinking that they don't all have to be there together, physically.

*Bolivian 182*: I see most of the Latino families are not happy. They live to work and pay the bills. Most of the people live for work. This is a change for us, because as a Latin, we live for our family. So we need to change our lifestyle, to live for work and to work a lot. That's why the families separate because we don't feel like a Latin again. It's a big part of our identity.

*Irish 140*: Families and communities mean very much to the Irish. But today the popular media—it's all about the big job, the promotion, the career. My children don't talk about community, they talk corporate stuff—advancing, being at the right place at the right time. This is their community. But if they have problems, is the corporation there to care for them the way the family and the community would have been? We've gone too far in that direction and people aren't making sense.

*Mexican 182*: As Mexicans, we want our children to stay with us until they marry. And we don't want them to move away when they have careers. But the colleges, they make it seem like the student should just get up and move away from family if they get a chance for a good job somewhere else. This is not the Mexican way—it's not the Latino way—but the kids listen to them, and now you see our communities breaking up because the kids think their professors know more than their parents. The kids say this is the American way. But what? To have a job making a few thousand dollars more, just to lose your family and friends and your ethnicity?

*Slovenian 155*: Slovenians never outgrow their families, and elders have a lot of influence over their grown children. For me personally, a big challenge was overcoming my parents' resistance to my moving out of their home during my college years.

On the other hand, some Milwaukee informants found ways to maintain solidarity with families and other ethnics through technology.

*Belgian 184*: When my company moved, I had to move. It took years to find anyone else from Belgium. Then some of us across the country with similar problems developed an email list.

*Scots Irish 160*: With email I started emailing my cousins every day. I used to see them every five or so years and maybe have one phone call a year on birthdays. Now it's every day. And in my search for my genealogy I found other lists of people from Appalachia and was able to connect to distant cousins and learn about them, which could never have happened without the Internet.

Hence, the American emphasis on upward mobility, which sometimes also translated into geographic mobility, was having a negative effect on ethnic solidarity. However, some in the Milwaukee sample found ways to soften it through email contact and email lists. Overcoming the cultural influence below was more challenging.

## Americanization and Child-rearing Practices

The cultural trend that informants mentioned most often as a threat to transmitting ethnic ways of life was contemporary child-rearing practices in the United States. According to Alba (1990, p. 164) the importance of child-rearing practices for ethnic groups in American society "is magnified by the comparative weakness of ethnicity in more public spheres, such as schools and workplaces." While ethnicity might have achieved a bit more attention in public spheres since 1990, the family still remains the chief vehicle for passing on traditions. Zhou (1997) argues that this is particularly important for children of underprivileged immigrant groups whose American socialization might come from the "culture of the young." Conversely, by adhering to the ethnic traditions of their parents they are more likely to develop forms of behavior that break the cycle of disadvantage and lead to upward mobility—practices such as hard work, willingness to take low-level jobs, and sacrifice for the future.

The Milwaukee informants underscored the importance of families' transmitting ethnic traditions to children. As in the case of mobility, most of the informants that expressed concerns about passing ethnic traditions to children were females under the age of fifty-five.

*German 144*: We've lost so much. Most have been here for six, seven generations. For a long time it was not popular to pass on ethnic ways to the kids and many did not. But now it's changed and we must be able to pass this on, or the ethnicity will be lost. So much has already been lost.

*Italian 187*: The kids now—the extended family to them was everything in those days. You saw those pictures. My God, look at my cousins. . . . See that's all gone. And with that goes the tradition, because the central institution of Italy is the family. And the family is the curator and the passer on-er of tradition. So once you don't have that anymore, people to remind you, you lose it. So that's why we have a problem here that all the other ethnic groups are having a problem with and that is getting the young people involved. Young people your age are [saying], "What's in it for me?"

*Jewish 153*: But it is interesting to reflect, as far as immigration, on how she [ancestor] wanted to leave all of her heritage behind, and totally become American. I think when you're thirteen, that's a very pivotal time, to make the decision to never, you know, speak Hebrew or Russian again. Or Yiddish was another one—from being in Poland—that was another language spoken within the family. She didn't want to speak any of those languages, really remember anything. And she was brought up in an Orthodox family and where there were lots of restrictions. So either you want to hold onto it (usually when you're an older person coming to this country, you know, preserve the heritage) or (when you're a younger one) you just want to completely adapt.

One of the barriers to passing on ethnic traditions that the Milwaukee informants discussed was the lack of time, both on the part of the children and on the part of the parents.

*Filipino 131*: It's [the family] pretty much Americanized, and I can say that based on what I've seen of friends and friends of friends. Many of our children, especially those born here, they can understand what you're saying, but they cannot speak the language. I have four kids and it's the case with them. Filipino language classes are pretty rare. They tried to offer it, but the demand was not there. The kids are busy. It's sad, but it's the truth. I've struggled with that too. I know I could do more to teach my kids, but it's a lot of work.

*Polish 137*: Times have changed. Once there were mothers who stayed at home. Now you rarely see this. Once you had an agrarian society where kids worked alongside the parents. Or there were family businesses. No more. There just is so little opportunity to teach some of the old world arts.

*Hmong 132*: Both have to work to pay the bills and put kids to school. A lot of parents today do not know the right way to help the kids, with peer influence, commercialism. Parents have very little time with the kids.

However, the main issue that the Milwaukee informants discussed was how little influence they felt they had over their children due to child-rearing practices in America—practices that had been slowly changing for decades. Popular parent-education literature since the 1930s advocated a more permissive and child-centered approach to training the young than in previous decades and was gradually replacing older literature that emphasized strict guidance and discipline. While some scholars (e.g., Gordon, 1968; Stendler, 1950) critiqued some of the parent-education literature and called for scientific evidence for any child-rearing approaches, the popular literature continued. In 1946, Benjamin Spock wrote *The Common Sense Book of Baby and Child Care,* which championed more relaxed, more affectionate child training practices, and sold more books in the twentieth century than any other than the Bible.

The trend in child-centered approaches culminated in the child rights dialogues of the 1970s. Richard Farson, a proponent of child rights in *Birthrights* (1974), never stated an age range for his definition of a "child," but argued that children should possess the same rights as adults in alternative home environments, access to information, educational choices, political and economic power, freedom from physical punishment, and "freedom for children to conduct their own sexual lives with no more restrictions than adults" (p. 152). The work never mentioned needs for children (or anyone) to learn from others' experiences or receive guidance from parents. Rather the entire thrust was on leveling the playing field between children and adults.

> The right to self-determination is the right to a single standard of morals and behavior for children and adults. . . . Children would have the right to engage in acts which are now acceptable for adults but not for children, and they would not be required to gain permission to do something if such permission is automatically granted to adults. (p. 27)

The United States never adopted this kind of bill of child rights, and American child-rearing culture never reached the extremes of the more extreme child-rights' advocates. However, research has shown that parents were losing control of children in urban areas where families had become more atomized (Bott, 1971), and problems emerged for new immigrant families when children expected parents to follow the American model (Waters, 1997). Most in the Milwaukee study described practices as more permissive than in their former homelands. Below, two first-generation Americans discuss the tight controls that their parents held over them.

> *Mexican 120*: We don't go out on our own. If you are a girl, you stay at home until you are married. Our parents go everywhere with us.

> *Burmese Mon 101*: You don't date people openly, and since you don't really date people outside of your own culture, then you don't see them often enough to get to know them. You don't move out until you get married. . . . I think that here in Milwaukee you Americans would go out on weekend days and people would go out to bars, but our culture—it's not open or maybe there are language barriers that make this hard, and stop us from going out and being more social with others. The Burmese refugees [Chin, Karen] would say that since the community is very small, and if a girl would go out a lot on her own, this is not looked good on or respected as much. It can be frustrating, and working five days a week and schooling, and sometimes you want to get away from the community, but you can't because your parents might not understand this as much.

The combination of parents having less time to spend with children and children expecting to make their own decisions ultimately dilutes the chances of parents in passing down ethnic traditions. When discussing the future of their ethnic practices, Milwaukee informants brought up these issues more often than any others under this category.

*Chinese 181*: My kids do really well, but inside my heart I want them to be a little more like Chinese thinking, but I can't push it. So I leave them. For example, parents cannot penalize the kids by spanking. In China that's common. I don't do that. I let them do whatever they want American style, but inside my heart I wish they could be more Chinese. . . . In China [the] individual is not important. The most important is the country, and then the family. Here it's the opposite.

*German 109*: I was a single parent and as such had less control over my children than most. In the days of my parents, we lived in ethnic neighborhoods and children with only one parent could rely on neighbors to help control the children. When I say control, I mean asking them to do the responsible things that would make them successful adults, but also passing on some of the German traditions that had been so carefully passed on to me and my brothers.

*African American 106*: We don't like being told how to raise our children. Today it's illegal to punish your child. How can you raise your kids up [in ways] that is right for your culture if you aren't allowed to raise them? Back in the day your neighbors would discipline your children if they did something bad. Today you just have to let them do what they want.

*Polish 135*: Everything changed in the seventies. That era changed the way we looked at things. You know, "Don't trust anyone over thirty." It pulled the young away from seniors and they did not socialize with older people anymore. That's where traditions ended. The Polish center and ethnic festivals had a lot to do with restoring some of this.

*Hmong 112*: Children [are] becoming so Americanized. The Lao that grew up here still believe in respect for the elders. But the younger generation has lost that respect. They don't like the traditional foods, and the parents can't change them anymore.

*Kashubian 102*: Kids were raised differently back then on the Island. They worked alongside the parents and did a lot of the same things. When we had free time we found fun things to do along the beach. Today the kids don't do that much with the parents because the parents have to be at work all the time. Parents don't really have any say.

The changes in child-rearing ideals since the middle of the twentieth century were clearly influencing the ability of groups to pass on ethnic ways. But ethnic groups are never static. For some, this influence propelled members to question the way they practiced some customs. For others, the influence drove them to re-emphasize long-established cultural values. See the field notes below.

*Field Notes: February, 2007*
The dinner at the Scandinavian center was well attended. While it went on for two hours, I arrived early, and sat with the 5:00 pm group, about 170 strong. The dinner was buffet style, with a variety of salads, drinks, main entrees (including boiled cod and Swedish meatballs), and desserts.

I took my place at a long table. Looking around I noticed that I was one of the younger people in the crowd (and I was over sixty). I asked a woman at the table if this was common.

"Sometimes you see a few families with children or some younger couples, but most of us that are involved are older." A man next to her (probably the husband) nodded his head in agreement.

I asked her if this was a problem.

"We think it is. It's so hard to get kids interested. There are a couple of women in the club who have started some youth programs, but getting kids to follow [in] their parents' footsteps is not easy these days."

*Field Notes: May, 2009*
A crowd of about 150 gathered outside the pavilion that housed the boxing club. They had come to celebrate the anniversary of the death of the club's former leader, an Ojibwe Indian elder. Many in the crowd were Ojibwe family members, some were supporters of the club, and others were neighborhood residents. As the crowd waited to enter the pavilion, youth from the boxing club walked down the line, politely welcoming each person to the ceremony. An apparently new club member lagged behind. The club's volunteer director, "John"—one of the sons of the Ojibwe being honored—ran up to the young member and instructed him to welcome people. "You want to show respect to these adults, the same way you would to your own grandmother. Now go down the line, welcome them to the ceremony, introduce yourself, and ask them if they need anything—water, a soda, any help." The new youth followed the instructions.

A couple from the neighborhood approached John and commended him on the respectful behavior of his kids.

"It's what we do here," John replied. "It's Indian ways, respecting elders."

At the door, other volunteers were smudging every member of the crowd with tobacco as they entered the pavilion—elders first.

# Addressing the Threats

The chapter discussed pressures that ethnic groups confronted in the recent past and pressures they continue to confront today. These included urban policies in the middle to late twentieth century that broke up ethnic neighborhoods and current trends in American culture that sometimes intervene in the transmission of ethnic ways.

In the middle to late twentieth century, two government-supported programs (often facilitated by private interests) played roles in disbanding ethnic neighborhoods in cities: urban renewal and freeway building. In urban areas across the nation, these programs razed ethnic neighborhoods that those in power deemed to be "blighted." In Milwaukee, the ethnic groups most affected by these programs included African Americans, Italians, Poles, Puerto Ricans, and Irish. Informants discussed effects on the health of their communities. African Americans described the loss of social organization—where dispersed families of strangers no longer watched over each other's children. They also lamented the removal of a once thriving business district that was never rebuilt. Italians and Puerto Ricans described the loss of core institutions that had once been the heart of their ethnic communities. And the Poles and Irish talked about the removal of housing that led to an early out-migration from their neighborhoods. While some groups managed to stay loosely connected in other areas of the city or just outside of Milwaukee, some groups worked to re-establish ethnic institutions in the old neighborhoods.

What individuals had lost in the dispersal was the close proximity to other ethnics—a proximity that helped to ensure the continuity of cultural patterns. As a result, ethnicity, where practiced, became more voluntary. It was something now *sought*, as opposed to being obligatory. The number of people strongly involved in ethnic practices may have diminished over time, but the personal commitment to these practices in the early twenty-first century was *intentional*.

However, other pressures continued to challenge ethnic solidarity, and the Milwaukee informants described these in the context of becoming "Americanized." To these informants, Americanization involved ideals associated with socioeconomic mobility or contemporary child rearing. Many indicated they were seeking upward mobility through education and employment, but experienced drawbacks when jobs and careers might require moving away from families and the ethnic community. On the other hand, some Milwaukee informants found ways to maintain solidarity with families and other ethnics through Internet communication.

The most trying challenge the Milwaukee informants described was passing on traditions to their children. In addition to the dwindling time available to teach children today when both parents were in the workforce, parents were also influenced by more permissive and child-centered approaches to training the young—approaches that put more emphasis on increasingly autonomous children choosing their own paths than following the traditions of past generations. Again, the groups were adapting. Some dealt with this challenge by creating special youth programs and others found ways to refocus the young on long-established cultural values.

The "Americanization" pressures the Milwaukee ethnics had been describing were those that were prevalent in a society that is highly individualistic—where the stress is on individual rights and opportunities, as opposed to duties toward collectivities. And it was the latter objective that the ethnic groups were actually carrying out, by nature of their practices.

## The Following Chapter

The concluding chapter will summarize the Milwaukee study and consider a new vision for ethnicity in America.

# Chapter Sixteen
# A New Vision for American Ethnicity

A new vision for American ethnicity is needed. While most ethnic scholars over the past century have attempted to explain how ethnicity benefits—or fails to benefit—*individuals,* few have focused on the community-contributing aspects of ethnic practices. There have been notable exceptions, including Greeley (1971), Salter (2002; 2004b), and Van der Dennen (2004) who argue that ethnic solidarity promotes public investment and is vital to the infrastructure of society. Countless others claim that ethnicity in America and elsewhere is either a nebulous concept or is divisive and used chiefly to promote individual self-interest. The Milwaukee study supports the arguments of the notable exceptions by showing how ethnic practices help restore the balance between individualism and collectivism in America—a country considered by some to be the most individualistic nation on earth (Hofstede, 1980).

## Ethnic Practices That Benefit Collectivities

The Milwaukee study, conducted between 2000 and the end of 2012, found that ethnic practices are still used to benefit individuals but also benefit collectivities, such as the family, neighborhood, town, and nation. Ethnicity has changed dramatically over the past century. Fewer people may be involved in ethnic practices than when families lived in ethnic enclaves, but ethnicity also became far more voluntary over the decades. Individuals in the early twenty-first century could select from multiple ethnic backgrounds and tended to choose ethnic activities that interested them and enhanced the quality of their lives. In many ways this made them better citizens.

## Improving Citizenship

Ethnic practices in the Milwaukee study fell under the categories of language and language retention, ties to past homelands, religion, food, art forms, healthcare and healing, genealogy, political activities, and work. More often than not, these practices were enriching and yielded outcomes such as increased knowledge of history; proficiency in languages other than English; involvement in visual, performance, and culinary arts; travel; knowledge of a body of healing practices and preventive health measures; and participation in sports and other health-promoting physical activities. These individual and group outcomes produced a more educated, well-rounded, and healthy American population. Add to this the variety of art forms, foods, dress styles, literature, and music genres (to name just a few) that ethnic practices generally contribute to American life, and the end product is more enriched families, neighborhoods, and municipalities.

But there are other ways that ethnic practices improve citizenship. Ethnicity, by definition, is oriented toward the past. Milwaukee informants were active seekers of ethnic history, often via genealogy research. Through oral and written family histories and examination of archival records, they captured a history "from below." Unwittingly, they became participants in movements to democratize history by unearthing the conditions on the ground while more powerful forces were reproducing versions from above. In some cases the information became transformational. By learning about tragedies, sacrifices, and deeds of their ancestors, some Milwaukee informants were able to put the present in perspective and become more appreciative of their current lives.

## Adding Community-serving Voluntary Associations

Another community-contributing practice of ethnic groups was the creation of voluntary associations. In Milwaukee County, the groups generated over 250 ethnic organizations. Much has been published about the benefits that rise from voluntary associations such as mitigating social isolation and contributing to democracy (e.g., Tocqueville, 2000; Eberly and Streeter, 2002). But it could be argued that the ethnic organizations described in the Milwaukee study provided even more wide-reaching contributions than typical voluntary associations. Most US voluntary associations tend to be oriented toward their membership (e.g., professional associations, special interest clubs) or a limited segment of the population (e.g., the disadvantaged, sick, men, women, families, elderly). But the functions of the ethnic associations were frequently all-embracing and added value to the community by offering services to ethnic members *and others in the wider society.* In Milwaukee County, these benefits included job training; voter registration drives; services that help families adapt to change; leisure time activities such as festivals, parades, picnics, and dinners; charitable functions for ethnic members and the community at large; and healthcare facilities.

## Making Needed Economic Contributions

Economic contributions are another outcome of ethnic practices. Ethnic informants in the Milwaukee study described how members of their families had filled economic niches by taking jobs that others could not or would not take, or how they opened businesses where they were needed. They described how their families' first generations in the United States worked long hours for low pay, and made sacrifices that would improve opportunities for the next generation. Often the work was dangerous and/or low in status, such as building the transcontinental railroad; janitorial services; working in mines, foundries, and tanneries; hotel service; asbestos abatement; food service; day care; opening grocery stores or gas stations in disadvantaged neighborhoods; domestic service; and filling temp jobs. Other informants described needed skills their families brought to the United States from their past homelands, including (to name only a few) tanning, glass blowing, metal work, printing, tool and die making, brewing, and ethnic culinary arts.

## Tolerance of Diversity

The 434 informants from over sixty ethnic groups in the Milwaukee study were those strongly involved in ethnic practices. Did this make them less or more tolerant of diversity? When asked what they liked about the Milwaukee area, the second most frequently coded response (behind size of metro area) was the cultural diversity. When the informants discussed other ethnic groups in the United States, most of their comments showed knowledge of the groups' cultures and histories, and tolerance (sometimes celebration) of their cultures. Negative comments were rare, and were made mostly by recent immigrants whose countries of origin may not have experienced the widespread changes in attitudes about diversity that the United States had. Others who sometimes expressed negative opinions lived in close proximity to other ethnic groups, where getting along often came down to questions such as: Did the groups support each other's agenda? Were some groups perceived as contributing to social disorganization? Did some appear less courteous and neighborly? However, even among informants living in close proximity to other groups, positive comments were more frequent than negative ones.

A question arises: Are individuals who are deeply involved in their own ethnic practices likely to be more tolerant—even appreciative—of other ethnic groups? The Milwaukee informants repeatedly expressed high opinions of other ethnic groups and general knowledge of their cultures and histories. Was this simply because they were interviewed during the post-civil rights era, or was this an outgrowth of the informants' profound involvement in their own American ethnic groups? The quotes presented throughout this book suggest the latter, but clearly more research is needed on this topic.

While the findings from this study may not fully support an assertion that individuals strongly involved in ethnic groups are likely to be more tolerant of cultural diversity than others, the clear findings in the qualitative descriptions of ethnic practices were the plethora of contributions that were being made to wider collectivities through these practices—whether the collectivity is the nation, town, neighborhood, or family. Ultimately these contributions strengthen the collectivities and help to support American society.

# New Directions for the Practice of Ethnicity

What movements are afoot that will strengthen ethnicity? What is still needed?

## DNA Research

DNA (deoxyribonucleic acid) was first extracted in 1984 from a mounted quagga, an extinct zebra. Since then, its uses have increased exponentially, including DNA studies involving ethnic origins and migrations (Kalb, 2006). Current DNA tests for individuals include Y chromosome, mitochondrial, and autosomal. The Y chromosome is passed from father to son. Daughters do not receive a Y chromosome. Y chromosomal DNA follows the direct paternal line (generally the surname line) indicating an ancestral location of the patriline such as Africa, Asia, or Europe. Mitochondrial DNA follows the maternal line in the same fashion, yielding the same types of information for the maternal mitochondrial line. Autosomal DNA, on the other hand, does not follow any line directly and is a composite of the information on the twenty-two autosomes contributed by both parents from all ancestors. Ethnicity information from autosomal DNA indicates a spectrum of results for the entire individual, not a single identification for one specific line—yielding results such as 10 percent African and 90 percent European. Together, these tests can provide information on ethnic ancestral composition, lineage migrations, biological traits, and disease risk. In addition, citizen scientists across the country are managing DNA projects on ethnic and subnational groups and publishing findings on topics such as ancestral origins and population variation. Some have even learned to conduct scientific experiments (Marcus, 2011).

The Melungeons of Appalachia project was an example of an important citizen scientist study (Estes, Goins, Ferguson, and Crain, 2011). In the past forty years, at least a score of books have been written about a "mysterious" population of dark-skinned Appalachians with uncertain ethnic and racial origins that once lived on mountain ridges in East Tennessee. They'd been tagged "the Melungeons" by neighboring communities. Speculation on the group's ethnic origins included (among others) Cherokee, Turkish, Gypsy, Jewish, Portuguese, and "Black Dutch." In 2011, a DNA study of known descendants of these Melungeons helped clear up the mystery. Their backgrounds were primarily Northern European and sub-Saharan African.

In the scholarly community, DNA studies involving race and ethnicity have thrived. While a few anthropologists and sociologists object to studies linking DNA to ethnicity—arguing that ethnicity is too fluid a human category for any kind of generalizations—others maintain that the studies can be used alongside other scientific programs to help clear up debates about topics such as population variation and ancient migrations (Bergisen, 2003). Some also use DNA to explore ways that environmental factors and interventions affect population health, by ethnic and racial group (Tadokoro et al., 2003). Together with archaeologists and historians, DNA scholars may eventually be able to chart "macro-identities" through historical stages, showing how ethnic populations migrated, related to resources, experienced contact with other populations, and adapted to change—a cultural model developed so well for Mexican Americans by Vigil (2012).

Ongoing DNA research on ethnicity will continue. It can only increase interest in the topic and help individuals better understand their ancestral origins.

## Ethnic Collaborations

Another movement that would help strengthen ethnicity is ethnic collaborations. Coalitions of multiple ethnic groups in the United States have been slow to develop. There have been efforts across the country to unite people of color under one umbrella (e.g., the Rainbow Coalition of Fred Hampton, and the Rainbow PUSH Coalition of Rev. Jesse Jackson), but few have attempted to unite a wider range of ethnic groups. In Milwaukee, Urban Anthropology Inc. organized an email list of twenty-four ethnic groups and a bimonthly newsletter called *Milwaukee Ethnic News*, but collaborative efforts failed to emerge from these endeavors. Attempts were sometimes thwarted by individuals not wishing to appear conciliatory toward a population that their group was in conflict with elsewhere, such as in the Middle East; at other times there simply was not an issue to unite enough groups.

Ethnic coalitions—both local and nation-wide—could be beneficial on many levels. They could address policies on topics such as immigration, civil rights, and cultural sensitivity in American institutions. They could help elect political candidates (Kopicki and Irving, 2012). They could impede movements that threatened ethnic neighborhoods such as those that prevailed during the widespread movement of populations during freeway building and urban renewal. Equally important, they could seek solutions to the more individualistic

threats the groups were facing, as found in the Milwaukee study. The most trying challenge the Milwaukee informants described was passing on traditions to
their children. In addition to the dwindling time available to teach children today
when both parents were in the workforce, parents were also influenced by more
permissive and child-centered approaches to training the young—approaches
that put more emphasis on increasingly autonomous children choosing their own
paths than following the traditions of past generations. Some groups in Milwaukee were finding solutions by creating special youth programs and others found
ways to refocus the young on long-established cultural values. These strategies
could be best discussed and developed in ethnic coalitions.

# The Future

By nature of their practices, ethnic groups have at times championed individual
rights and opportunities. But the Milwaukee study demonstrates that their practices also contribute much to the wider US society, helping to restore the balance
between individualism and collectivism. Any new vision for ethnicity in America should be one that promotes ethnic involvement. The United States has come
a long way from the melting pot manifesto that pressured groups to assimilate to
an Anglo-American ideal to today's tolerance for diversity. As Yinger (1994)
asserted, it is no longer a case of assimilation versus ethnicity but of assimilation
and ethnicity. The need now is to move beyond merely honoring diversity to the
point where American institutions promote ethnic involvement for the well-
being of the family, the neighborhood, the town, and the nation.

# Appendix

## List of Interviewees

*Note:* The total number of interviews conducted in the Milwaukee study was 438. However, four interviewees were interviewed for two ethnic groups each, in which they claimed strong participation; hence the total number of interviewees was 434.

Ethnic self-identification of interviewees claiming ancestors that emigrated from Europe (n=252):

Bulgarian (1), Czech (2), Danish (1), Dutch (2), English (14), Flemish/Belgian (2), French (15), German (36), German Russian (4), Greek (8), Hungarian (2), Irish (30), Italian (29), Jewish (13), Kashubian (9), Latvian (1), Lithuanian (1), Luxembourgish (1), Norwegian (14), Polish (32), Russian (9), Scottish (4), Scots Irish (3), Serbian (5), Slovak (2), Slovenian (7), Spanish (1), Swedish (2), Swiss (1), Welsh (1)

Ethnic self-identification of interviewees claiming ancestors that emigrated from Africa (n=54):

African American (42), Bantu (1), Black Muslim (1), Congolese (1), Ibo (1), Kurian (2), Malinke (1), Mbere (1), Mina (1), Somali (2), Yoruba (1)

Ethnic self-identification of interviewees claiming ancestors that emigrated from Asia and the Middle East (n=47):

Arab (3), Burmese/Mon (1), Chinese (4), Filipino (3), Hmong (14), Indian (2), Japanese (1), Jewish (3), Korean (2), Nepali (1), Pakistani (1), Palestinian (4), Russian (4), Taiwanese (2), Turk (2)

Ethnic self-identification of interviewees claiming ancestors that emigrated from indigenous North America (n=29):

> Cherokee (1), Cree (1), Creek (1), Ho Chunk (3), Lakota (1), Menominee (4), Ojibwe (8), Oneida (5), Potawatomi (3), Stockbridge Munsee (2)

Ethnic self-identification of interviewees claiming ancestors that emigrated from Latin America (including the Caribbean) (n=56):

> Bolivian (1), Chilean (2), Cuban (2), Dominican (2), Haitian (1), Mexican (34), Peruvian (2), Puerto Rican (9), Salvadorian (2), Venezuelan (1)

# Checklist for Ethnic Participation

*Note*: Interviewers queried potential informants for ethnic involvement via a checklist (unless the information was already known to the interviewer). To be considered an informant for an ethnic group, the person had to be involved in at least half of the following activities.

1. Can read and/or converse in one of the languages of the former homeland of ethnic group
2. Is a participating member of an organization of the ethnic group
3. Has visited a former homeland
4. Practices one of the major religions of ethnic group
5. Routinely eats the traditional foods of ethnic group
6. Engages in an art form specific to the ethnic group (e.g., music, dance, visual arts, theatre, textiles, stories, literature)
7. Is active in advocating for policies that help ethnic group and/or its former homeland
8. Employment or business (whether part time or full time) involves products and/or services of ethnic group
9. Engages in genealogy or history to learn about ethnic ancestors
10. Attends at least two public events each year to celebrate ethnic heritage

# Interviewing Schedule (2000 thru 2012)

*Note:* In most cases the scheduling of ethnic groups to be interviewed and observed followed the interests of the anthropologists and interns.

- 2000-2002: The research team interviewed and observed the African Americans, Irish, and Poles.
- 2000-2004: The research team interviewed and observed the North American Indians, Kashubes, and Hmong.
- 2005-2006: The research team interviewed and observed the French, Germans, and all Latin American groups.
- 2007-2008: The research team interviewed and observed the Italians, Serbs, all Scandinavian groups, and the remaining Slavic groups.
- 2009-2010: The research team interviewed and observed the African groups, Greeks, English, and the remaining European groups.
- 2011-end of 2012: During the last two years, all remaining groups in Asia and the Middle East were interviewed. During this time, the team also sought out informants from ethnic groups that had been missed and contacted leaders of the groups interviewed earlier for names of potential new informants or events to be observed.

# Bibliography

Alba, R. D. (1985). *Italian Americans: Into the twilight of ethnicity.* Englewood Cliffs, NJ: Prentice Hall.

————— (1990). *Ethnic identity: The transformation of white America.* New Haven, CT: Yale University Press.

American Jewish Committee. (2005). *Annual survey of American-Jewish opinion.* New York, NY: AJC.

Anderson, B. (1991). *Imagined communities: Reflections on the origin and spread of nationalism.* London, England: Verso.

Anderson, E. N. (1997). Traditional medical values of food. In C. Counihan, & P. Van Esterik (Eds.), *Food and culture: A reader* (pp. 80-91). New York, NY: Routledge.

Aponte-Pares, L. (2000). Appropriating place in Puerto Rican Barrios: Preserving contemporary urban landscapes. In A. R. Alanen, & R. Z. Melnick (Eds.), *Preserving Cultural Landscapes in America* (94-111). Baltimore, MD: The Johns Hopkins University Press.

Banks, M. (1996). *Ethnicity: Anthropological constructions.* London, England: Routledge.

Banton, M. (1983). *Racial and ethnic competition.* Cambridge, England: Cambridge University Press.

Barth, F. (1966). *Models of social organization.* London, England: Royal Anthropologist Institute of Great Britain and Ireland.

————— (1970). Introduction. In F. Barth (Ed.), *Ethnic groups and boundaries* (9-38). London, England: George Allen & Unwin.

Bell, D. (1975). Ethnicity and social change. In N. Glazer, & D. P. Moynihan (Eds.), *Ethnicity: Theory and experience* (pp. 141-176). Cambridge: Harvard University Press.

Bergisen, U. (2003). Using DNA to help solve the riddle of ancient Germanic migration. *Mankind Quarterly, 4*(1), 91-109.

Bernard, H. R. (2006). *Research methods in anthropology: Qualitative and quantitative approaches* (4th ed.). Lanham, MD: AltaMira.

Bott, E. (1971). *Family and social network: Roles, norms and external relationships in ordinary urban families.* London, England: Tavistock.

Brislin, R. W. (1981). *Cross-cultural encounters: Face to face interaction.* New York, NY: Pergamon Press.

Burnham, L. F. (1994). Tyranny from the tyrannized. *Utne Reader, 61,* 133-135.

Clarke, C., Ley, D., & Peach, C. (1984). Introduction. In C. Clarke, D. Ley, & C. Peach (Eds.), *Geography and ethnic pluralism* (pp. 1-20). London, England: George Allen & Unwin.

143

Cohen, A. (1974a). *Two-dimensional man: An essay on the anthropology of power and symbolism in complex societies.* Berkeley: University of California Press.

Cohen, A. (1974b). Introduction. In A. Cohen (Ed.), *Urban ethnicity* (pp. ix-xxiv). London, England: Tavistock.

Cohen, A. P. (1994) *Self-consciousness: An alternative anthropology of identity.* London, England: Routledge.

Cohen, D. S. (1998). Reflections on American ethnicity. In J. Ferrante, & P. Brown (Eds.), *The social construction of race and ethnicity in the United States* (239-248). New York, NY: Longman.

Corbett, J. M. (1997). *Religion in America* (3rd ed.). Upper Saddle River, NJ: Prentice Hall.

Cornell, S. (1996). The variable ties that bind: Content and circumstance in ethnic processes. *Ethnic and Racial Studies, 19,* 265-289.

Cornell, S., & Hartmann, D. (2007). *Ethnicity and race: Making identities in a changing world.* Thousand Oaks, CA: Pine Forge Press.

Crevecoeur, M. G. (1782). *Letters from an American farmer: Describing certain provincial situations, manners, and customs, not generally known; and conveying some idea of the late and present interior circumstances of the British colonies of North America.* London, England.

Demaine, H. (1984). Furnivall reconsidered: Plural societies in South-East Asia in the post colonial era. In C. Clarke, D. Ley, & C. Peach (Eds.), *Geography and ethnic pluralism* (pp. 25-50). London: George Allen & Unwin.

Denzin, N. K., & Lincoln, Y. S. (Eds.). (2005). *Handbook of qualitative research* (3rd ed.). Thousand Oaks, CA: Sage.

Despres, L. A. (1975). Toward a theory of ethnic phenomena. In L. A. Despres (Ed.), *Ethnicity and resource competition in plural societies* (pp. 187-208). Chicago, IL: Mouton.

Devons, E., & Gluckman, M. (1964). Conclusion: Modes and consequences of limiting a field of study. In M. Gluckman (Ed.), *Closed systems and open minds. The limits of naivety in social anthropology* (pp. 158-262). Hawthorne, NY: Aldine.

De Vos, G. A. (1975). Ethnic pluralism: Conflict and accommodation. In G. A. De Vos, & L. Romanucci-Ross (Eds.), *Ethnic identity: Cultural continuities and change* (pp. 5-41). Palo Alto, CA: Mayfield.

DeVos, G. A. (1998). Confucian family socialization: The religion, morality, and aesthetics of property. In W. H. Slate, & G. A. DeVos (Eds.), *Confucianism and the family* (pp. 329-380). Albany: State University of New York Press.

Dluhy, M., Revell, K., & Wong, S. (2002). Creating a positive future for a minority community: Transportation and urban renewal politics in Miami. *Journal of Urban Affairs, 24*(1), 75-95.

Duncan, O. D., & Duncan, B. (1955). Residential distribution and occupational stratification. *American Journal of Sociology, 60,* 493-503.

Duncan, O. D., & Lieberson, S. (1959). Ethnic segregation and assimilation. *American Journal of Sociology, 64,* 364-374.

Durarte, E. M., & Smith, S. (2000). *Foundational perspectives in multicultural education.* New York, NY: Longman.

Eberly, D., & Streeter, R. (2002). *The soul of civil society: Voluntary associations and the public value of moral habits.* Lanham, MD: Lexington Books.

Eibl-Eibesfeldt, I. (2004). Ethnicity, the problem of differential altruisms, and international multiculturalism. In Frank Salter (Ed.), *Welfare, ethnicity and altruism: New findings and evolutionary theory* (pp. 283-291). London, England: Frank Cass.

Emerson, R. W. (1912). *Journals of Ralph Waldo Emerson with annotations* (Vol. 3). Ann Arbor: University of Michigan Library.

Epstein, A. L. (1978). *Ethos & identity: Three studies in ethnicity*. London, England: Tavistock.

Eriksen, T. H. (2003). *Ethnicity and nationalism* (2nd ed.). London, England: Pluto Press.

Espiritu, Y. L. (2001). Theories of ethnicity: An overview and assessment. In J. Ferrante, & P. Browne (Eds.), *The social construction of race and ethnicity in the United States* (2nd ed.) (pp. 257-263). Upper Saddle River, NJ: Prentice Hall.

Estes, R. J., Goins, J. H., Ferguson, P., & Crain, J. L. (2011). Melungeons: A multi-ethnic population. *Journal of Genetic Genealogy*, 7. Retrieved from http://www.jogg.info/72/index.html

Evans-Cowley, J. S., & Nasar, J. L. (2003). Signs as yard art in Amarillo, Texas. *The Geographical Review, 93*(1), 97-115.

Farb, P., & Armelagos, G. (1980). *Consuming passions: The anthropology of eating*. New York, NY: Washington Square Press.

Farley, R., & Alba, R. (2002). The new second generation in the United States. *International Migration Review, 36*(3), 669-701.

Farson, R. (1974). *Birthrights*. Middlesex, England: Penguin Books.

Feliciano, C. (2006, May). Another way to assess the second generation: Look at the parents. *Migration Information Source*. Migration Policy Institute. Retrieved from http://www.migrationinformation.org/feature/display.cfm?ID=396

Ferraro, G. (1998). *Cultural anthropology: An applied perspective*. Belmont, CA: West/Wadsworth.

Firth, R. (1989). Fiction and fact in ethnography. In E. Tonkin, M. McDonald, & M. Chapman (Eds.), *History and ethnicity* (pp. 48-52). London, England: Routledge.

Fischer, C. (1975). Toward a subcultural theory of urbanism. *American Journal of Sociology, 80*, 1319-1341.

Foster, G. M., & Kemper, R. V. (1974). Introduction. In G. M. Foster, & R. V. Kemper (Eds.), *Anthropologists in cities* (pp. 1-18). Boston, MA: Little, Brown & Co.

Friedl, J., & Chrisman, N. J. (1975). Introduction. In J. Friedl, & N. J. Chrisman (Eds.), *City ways: A selective reader in urban anthropology* (pp. 1-25). New York, NY: Thomas Y. Crowell.

Furnival, J. S. (1948). *Colonial policy and practice: A comparative study of Burma and Netherlands India*. Cambridge, England: Cambridge University Press.

Gans, H. (1979). Symbolic ethnicity: The future of ethnic groups and cultures in America. *Ethnic and Racial Studies, 2*(1), 1-20.

Gans, H. (1992). Second generation decline: Scenarios for the American immigrants. *Ethnic and Racial Studies, 15*(2), 173-192.

——— (1999). *Making sense of America: Social analyses and essays*. Lanham, MD: Rowman & Littlefield.

Geertz, C. (1963). Religion as a cultural system. In M. Banton (Ed.), *Anthropological approaches to the study of religion* (pp. 1-46). New York, NY: Frederick A. Praeger.

——— (1973). *The interpretation of cultures*. New York, NY: Basic Books.

Gellner, E. (1995). *Anthropology and politics: Revolutions in the sacred grove*. Oxford, England: Blackwell.

Gioielle, R. (2011). We must destroy you to save you. *Radical History Review, 109*, 62-82.

Glazer, N., & Moynihan, D. P. (1970). *Beyond the melting pot: The Negros, Puerto Ricans, Jews, Italians, and Irish of New York City* (2nd ed.). Cambridge, MA: MIT Press.

Glazer, N. (1997). *We are all multiculturalists now.* Cambridge, MA: Harvard University Press.

Gold, S. J. (2006, October). The second generation and self employment. *Migration Information Source.* Migration Policy Institute. Retrieved from http://www. migrationinformation.org/Feature/display.cfm?ID=447

Gonzales, N. A., & Cause, A. M. (1995). Ethnic identity and multicultural competence: Dilemmas and challenges. In W. D. Hawley, & A. W. Jackson (Eds.), *Toward a common destiny: Improving race and ethnic relations in America* (pp. 131-162). San Francisco, CA: Jossey-Bass.

Goodenough, W. (1970). Describing a culture. In W. Goodenough & A. Harris (Eds.), *Description and comparison in cultural anthropology* (pp. 104-119). Cambridge, England: Cambridge University Press.

Gordon, M. (1968). Infant care revisited. *Journal of Marriage and the Family, 10,* 548-583.

Gordon, M. M. (1964). *Assimilation in American life: The role of race, religion, and national origins.* New York, NY: Oxford University Press.

Greeley, A. M. (1971). *Why can't they be like us? America's white ethnic groups.* New York, NY: E.P. Dutton.

————— (1974). *Ethnicity in the United States: A preliminary reconnaissance.* New York, NY: John Wiley & Sons.

————— (1981). *The Irish Americans: The rise to money and power.* New York, NY: Harper & Row.

Gurda, J. (1999). *The making of Milwaukee.* Milwaukee: Milwaukee County Historical Society.

Hannerz, U. (1974). *Soulside: Inquiries into ghetto culture and community.* New York, NY: Columbia University Press.

————— (1974). Ethnicity and opportunity in urban America. In A. Cohen (Ed.), *Urban ethnicity* (pp. 37-76). London, England: Tavistock.

Hansen, M. L. (1952, November 14). The third generation in America. *Commentary,* pp. 493-500. Retrieved from http://www.commentarymagazine.com/article/the-study-of-man-the-third-generation-in-america/

Heller, M. (1987). The role of language in the formation of ethnic identity. In J. S. Phinney and M. J. Rotheram (Eds.), *Children's ethnic socialization: Pluralism and development* (pp. 180-200). Newbury Park, CA: Sage.

Helman, C. G. (2001). *Culture, health and illness.* London: Arnold.

Herskovitz, M. (1941). *The myth of the Negro past.* New York, NY: Harper Brothers.

Hicks, G. L. (1977). Introduction: Problems in the study of ethnicity. In G. L. Hicks, & P. E. Leis (Eds.), *Ethnic encounters: Identity and context* (pp. 1-20). North Scituate, MA: Duxbury Press.

Highsmith, A. R. (2009). Demolition means progress: Urban renewal, local politics, and state-sanctioned ghetto formation in Flint, Michigan. *Journal of Urban History, 35,* 348-368.

Hill, J. D. (2000). *Becoming a cosmopolitan: What it means to be a human being in the new millennium.* Lanham, MD: Rowman & Littlefield.

Hirschfeld, L. A. (1996). *Race in the making: Cognition, culture, and the child's construction of human kinds.* Cambridge, MA: MIT Press.

Ho, D. (Ed.) (1979). *Psychological implications of collectivism: With special reference to the Chinese case and Maoist dialectics.* Amsterdam, Holland: Swets & Zeitlinga.

Hoddie, M. (2006). *Ethnic realignments: A comparative study of government influences on identity.* Lanham, MD: Lexington Books.

Hofstede, G. (1980). *Culture's consequences.* Beverly Hills, CA: Sage.

Holtorf, C. (2012). The heritage of heritage. *Heritage & Society, 2,* 153-174.

Holtzman, J. D. (2006). Food and memory. *Annual Review of Anthropology, 36,* 371-378.

Hopper, P. (2003). *Rebuilding communities in an age of individualism.* Burlington, VT: Ashgate.

How popular is genealogy? (2009, February). *Eastman's Online Genealogy Newsletter.* Retrieved from http://blog.eogn.com/eastmans_online_genealogy/2009/02 /how-popular-is-genealogy.html

Howard, C. (2007). Introduction. In C. Howard (Ed.), *Contested individualization: Debates about contemporary personhood.* New York, NY: Palgrave MacMillan.

Humphrey, T. C., & Humphrey, L. T. (1991). *"We gather together": Food and festival in American life.* Logan: Utah State University Press.

Hunt, C., & Walker, L. (1974). *Ethnic dynamics: Patterns of intergroup relations in various societies.* Homewood, IL: The Dorsey Press.

Ignatiev, N. (2009). *How the Irish became white.* New York, NY: Routledge.

Jacobson, M. F. (1998). *Whiteness of a different color: European immigrants and the alchemy of race.* Cambridge, MA: Harvard University Press.

——— (2006). *Roots too: White ethnic revival in post-civil rights America.* Cambridge, MA: Harvard University Press.

Jansen, C. (1999, November 10). Freeways paved way but ran over neighborhoods. *Journal Sentinel,* pp. A1, A6.

Jellema, K. (2007). Everywhere incense burning: Remembering ancestors in Dol Moi Vietnam. *Journal of Southeast Asian Studies, 38*(3). Retrieved from http://www. questia.com/library/1G1-171295976/everywhere-incense-burning-remembering-ancestors

Jenkins, R. (1984). Overview. Ethnic minorities in business: A research agenda. In R. Ward, & R. Jenkins (Eds.), *Ethnic communities in business: Strategies for economic survival* (pp. 231-238). Cambridge, England: Cambridge University Press.

Jenkins, W. D. (2001). Before downtown: Cleveland, Ohio and urban renewal, 1949-1958. *Journal of Urban History, 27,* 471-496.

Jones, E. M. (2004). *The slaughter of cities: Urban renewal as ethnic cleansing.* South Bend, IN: St. Augustine's Press.

Kalb, C. (2006, February). In our blood: DNA testing: It is connecting lost cousins and giving families surprising glimpses into their pasts. *Newsweek.* Retrieved from http://www.questia.com/library/1G1-141452331/in-our-blood-dna-testing-it-is-connecting-lost-cousins

Kalcik, S. (1984). Foodways in America: Symbol and the performance of identity. In L. K. Brown, & K. Mussell (Eds.), *Ethnic and regional foodways in the United States: The performance of group identity* (pp. 37-65). Knoxville: University of Tennessee Press.

Kallen, H. (1970). *Culture and democracy in the United States.* New York, NY: Arno Press & the New York Times.

Karner, C. (2007). *Ethnicity and everyday Life.* London, England: Routledge.

Kendall, L. (2001). Encounters with Korean ancestors: Rituals, dreams, and stories. In S. Friesen (Ed.), *Ancestors in post-contact religion: Roots, ruptures, and modernity's memory* (pp. 135-156). Cambridge, MA: Harvard University Press.

Kennett, D. (2011). *DNA and social networking: A guide to genealogy in the twenty-first century.* Gloucestershire, England: The History Press.

Kopicki, A., & Irving, W. (2012, November 20). Assessing how pivotal the Hispanic vote was to Obama's victory. *The New York Times.* Retrieved from http://thecaucus.blogs.nytimes.

com/2012/11/20/assessing-how-pivotal-the-hispanic-vote-was-to-obamas-victory/?emc=
etal
Lackey, J. F. (Urban Anthropology). (2006). *The cultural roots of Milwaukee's Socialist
movement* [DVD]. Available from http://www.urban-anthropology.org
Lal, B. B. (1990). *The romance of culture in an urban civilization: Robert E. Park on race and
ethnic relations in cities.* London, England: Routledge.
Lavine, A. (2012). Urban renewal and the story of Berman v. Parker. *The Urban Lawyer,
42*(2), 423-475.
Lee, M. L., & Sun, T. H. (1995). The family and demography in contemporary Taiwan.
*Journal of Comparative Family Studies, 26,* 101-115.
Levine, H. (1997). *Constructing collective identity: A comparative analysis of New Zealand
Jews, Maori, and urban Papua New Guineans.* Frankfurt, Germany: Main: Peter Lang.
Lewis, G. (2001). Health: An elusive concept. In H. Macbeth, & P. Shetty (Vol. Eds.), *Society
for the study of human biology series: Vol. 41. Health and Ethnicity* (pp. 59-67). London:
Taylor & Francis.
Lewis, H. S. (1974). European ethnicity in Wisconsin: An exploratory formulation. *Ethnicity,
5,* 174-188.
Lewis, O. (1952). Urbanism without breakdown: A case study. *Scientific Monthly, 75,* 31-41.
Lieberson, S. (1963). *Ethnic patterns in American cities.* New York, NY: The Free Press of
Glenco.
——— (1970). *Language and ethnic relations in Canada.* New York, NY: John Wiley &
Sons.
Lind, R. (2007). *The seat of consciousness in ancient literature.* Jefferson, NC: McFarland.
Little, K. (1973). *African women in towns: An aspect of African social revolution.* Cambridge,
England: Cambridge University Press.
——— (1974). *Urbanization as a social process: An essay on movement and change in
contemporary Africa.* London, England: Routledge.
Little, K. L. (1958). *Race and society.* Paris, France: UNESCO.
Marcus, A. D. (2011, December 3). The Saturday essay: Citizen scientists. *Wall Street
Journal.* Retrieved from http://online.wsj.com/article/SB 10001424052970204621904
577014330551132036.html
Mayer, P. (1961). *Townsmen or tribesmen: Conservatism and the process of urbanization in a
South African city.* Cape Town, South Africa: Oxford University Press.
Migration & Remittances (2013). *Topics in development.* Retrieved from http://web.world
bank.org/WBSITE/EXTERNAL/TOPICS/0,,contentMDK:21924020~pagePK:5105988~
piPK:360975~theSitePK:214971,00.html
Mintz, S. W., & Du Bois, C. M. (2002). The anthropology of food and eating. *Annual Review
of Anthropology, 31,* 99-119.
Nagel, J. (1998). Resource competition theories. In J. Ferrante, & P. Brown (Eds.), *The social
construction of race and ethnicity in the United States* (pp. 249-267). New York, NY:
Longman.
Narroll, R. (1964). Ethnic unit classification. *Current Anthropology, 5*(4), 282-312.
National Conference of Christians and Jews. (1994). *Taking America's pulse.* New York, NY:
NCC.
Noble, A. G. (1992). *To build a new land: Ethnic landscapes in North America.* Baltimore,
MD: The Johns Hopkins University Press.
Novak, M. (1975). *The rise of the unmeltable ethnics: Politics and culture in the seventies.*
New York, NY: Maxmilian.

Pager, D. (2007). *Marked: Race, crime, and finding work in an era of mass incarceration.* Chicago. IL: University of Chicago Press.

Paradis, T. K. (2006). *German Milwaukee: Its history—its recipes.* St. Louis, MO: G. Bradley.

Park, R. E., & Burgess, E. W. (1966). *Introduction to the science of sociology* (3rd ed.). Chicago, IL: University of Chicago Press.

Pate, D. (2011, July 16). Let's help ex-prisoners find work. *JS Online: Milwaukee Journal Sentinel.* Retrieved from http://www.jsonline.com/news/opinion/ 125668533.html

Patterson, O. (1977). *Ethnic chauvinism: The reactionary impulse.* New York, NY: Stein & Day.

Patton, M. Q. (2002). *Qualitative research & evaluation methods* (3rd ed.). Thousand Oaks, CA: Sage.

Peroff, N. (2001). Indianness. In J. Ferrante and P. Browne (Eds.), *The social construction of race and ethnicity in the United States* (2nd ed.) (pp. 427-428). Upper Saddle River, NJ: Prentice Hall.

Powdermaker, H. (1968). *After freedom: A cultural study in the Deep South.* New York, NY: Russell & Russell.

Redfield, R. (1941). *The folk culture of the Yucatan.* Chicago, IL: University of Chicago Press.

Rex, J. (1986). *Race and ethnicity.* Milton Keynes, England: Open University Press.

Roosens, E. E. (1989). *Creating ethnicity: The process of ethnogenesis.* Newbury Park, CA: Sage.

Rosenblatt, R. (1999). Introduction. In R. Rosenblatt (Ed.), *Consuming desires: Consumption, culture, and the pursuit of happiness* (pp. 1-24). Washington, DC: Island Press.

Rubel, A. J., & Hass, M. R. (1990). Ethnomedicine. In T. M. Johnson, & C. F. Sargent (Eds.), *Medical anthropology: Contemporary theory and method.* New York, NY: Praeger.

Said, E. (1978). *Orientalism.* London, England: Routledge & Kegan Paul.

Salter, F. (2004a). Ethnic diversity, foreign and economic growth, population policy, welfare, inequality, conflict, and costs of globalism: A perspective on W. Masters' and M. McMillan 's findings. In F. Salter (Ed.), *Welfare, ethnicity and altruism: New findings and evolutionary theory* (pp. 148-170). London, England: Frank Cass.

———— (2004b). The evolutionary deficit in mainstream political theory of welfare and ethnicity. In F. Salter (Ed.), *Welfare, ethnicity and altruism: New findings and evolutionary theory* (pp. 306-327). London, England: Frank Cass.

———— (2002). Introduction: From mafia to freedom fighters: Questions raised by ethology and sociobiology. In F. K. Salter (Ed.), *Risky transactions: Trust, kinship and ethnicity* (pp. 3-20). New York, NY: Gerghahn Books.

Sandberg, N. C. (1964). *Ethnic identity and assimilation: The Polish-American community.* New York, NY: Oxford University Press.

Sanders, G. (2000). A black perspective on the gathering place by the rivers. In K. Little (Ed.), *The state of black Milwaukee* (pp. 35-38). Milwaukee, WI: Milwaukee Urban League.

Sanders, J. M. (2002). Ethnic boundaries and identity in plural societies. *Annual Review of Sociology, 28,* 327-357.

Sardar, Z. (1999). *Orientalism.* Buckingham, England: Open University Press.

Schaefer, R. T. (2007). *Race and ethnicity in the United States* (11th ed.). Upper Saddle River, NJ: Pearson, Prentice Hall.

Schnell, S. M. (2003). Creating narratives of place and identity in "Little Sweden, U.S.A." *The Geographical Review, 93*(1), 1-20.

Sherman, S. R. (1991). The Passover seder: Ritual dynamics, foodways, and family folklore. In Humphrey, L. T. & Humphrey, T. C. (Eds.), *"We gather together": Food and festival in American life* (pp. 27-42). Logan: Utah State University Press.

Sheskin, I. M. (1996). *Jewish community study: Main report.* Milwaukee: Milwaukee Jewish Federation.

Shils, E. (1957). Primordial, personal, sacred and civil ties. *British Journal of Sociology, 8*(2), 130-145.

——— (1968). Color, the universal intellectual community, and the Afro-Asian intellectual. In J. H. Franklin (Ed.), *Color and race* (pp. 1-17). Boston, MA: Houghton Mifflin.

Smith, A. D. (1981). *The ethnic revival.* Cambridge, England: Cambridge University Press.

Smith, M. G. (1984). *Culture, race and class in the Commonwealth Caribbean.* Mona, Jamaica: Institute of Social and Economic Research.

——— (1986). Pluralism, race and ethnicity in selected African countries. In J. Rex, & D. Mason (Eds.), *Theories of race and ethnic relations* (pp. 187-225). Cambridge, England: Cambridge University Press.

Smith, N. (2012, September). The new American dream: Fame & fortune. *Business News.* Retrieved from http://www.businessnewsdaily.com/3170-american-dream-evolving.html

Spock, B. (1946). *The common sense book of baby and child care.* New York, NY: Pocket Books.

Spradley, J. P. (1979). *The ethnographic interview.* Belmont, CA: Wadsworth.

——— (1980). *Participant observation.* New York: Holt, Rinehart, and Winston.

Steadman, L. B., Palmer, C. T., & Tilley, C. F. (2002). The universality of ancestor worship. *Ethnology, 35*(1), 63-80.

Steinberg, S. (2001). *The ethnic myth* (3rd ed.). Boston, MA: Beacon Press.

Stendler, C. (1950). Sixty years of child training practices. *Journal of Pediatrics, 36,* 122-134.

Sutton, D. E. (2001). *Remembrance of repasts: An anthropology of food and memory.* New York, NY: Oxford Press.

Tadokoro, T., Kobayashi, N., Zmudzka, B. Z., Ito, S., Wakamatsu, K., Yamaguchi, Y., Korossy, K. S., Miller, S. A., Beer, J. Z., & Hearing, V. J. (2003). UV-induced DNA damage and melanin content in human skin differing in racial/ethnic origin. *The FASEB Journal, 17*(9), 1177-1179.

Teaford, J. C. (1990). *The rough road to renaissance: Urban revitalization in America, 1940-1985.* Baltimore, MD: The Johns Hopkins University Press.

Thomas, W. I., & Znaniecki, F., (1984). *The Polish peasant in Europe and America.* Urbana: University of Illinois Press.

Tocqueville, Alexis de (2000). *Democracy in America.* Chicago, IL: The University of Chicago Press.

Tolan, T. (2003). *Riverwest: A community history.* Milwaukee, WI: COA.

Tolan, T., & Glauber, B. (2010, December 14). Milwaukee area tops Brookings segregation study of census data. *Milwaukee Journal Sentinel.* Retrieved from http://www.js-online.com/news/milwaukee/111898689.html

Tonkin, E., McDonald, M., & Chapman, M. (1989). Introduction: History and social anthropology. In E. Tonkin, M. McDonald, & M. Chapman (Eds.), *History and ethnicity* (pp. 1-21). London, England: Routledge.

Toussaint-Samat, M. (2009). *A history of food: New expanded edition.* Oxford, England: Wiley-Blackwell.

Triandis, H. C. (1995). *Individualism and collectivism.* Boulder, CO: Westview Press.

Trotter, R. T., II, & Chavira, J. A. (1997). *Curanderismo: Mexican American folk healing* (2nd ed.). Athens: University of Georgia Press.

Turner, F. J. (1893, July). *The significance of the frontier in American history.* Symposium conducted at the meeting of the American Historical Association, Chicago, IL.

———— (1958). *The frontier in American history.* New York, NY: Henry Holt.

Van den Berghe, P. L. (1981). *The ethnic phenomenon.* New York, NY: Elsevier.

———— (1986). Ethnicity and the socio-biology debate. In J. Rex, & D. Mason (Eds.), *Theories of race and ethnic relations* (pp. 246-263). Cambridge, England: Cambridge University Press.

Van der Dennen, J. M. G. (2004). Selfish co-operation, loyalty structures, and proto-ethnocentrism in inter-group agonistic behavior. In F. Salter (Ed.), *Welfare, ethnicity and altruism: New findings and evolutionary theory* (pp. 195-231). London, England: Frank Cass.

Vigil, J. D. (2012). *From Indians to Chicanos: The dynamics of Mexican-American culture* (3rd ed.). Long Grove, IL: Waveland.

Vinson, T. S., & Neimeyer, G. J. (2000). The Relationship between racial identity development and multicultural counseling competency. *Journal of Multicultural Counseling and Development, 28*(3), 127-192.

Waldinger, R. (1997). Black/immigrant competition re-assessed: New evidence from Los Angeles. *Sociological Perspectives, 40*, 365-386.

Waller, J. (2000). *Prejudice across America.* Jackson: University Press of Mississippi.

Wallman, S. (1979). Introduction. In S. Wallman (Ed.), *Ethnicity at work* (pp. 1-16). London, England: Macmillan Press.

Warner, W. L., & Srole, L. (1945). *The social systems of American ethnic groups.* New Haven: Yale University Press.

Waters, M. C. (1990). *Ethnic options: Choosing identities in America.* Berkeley: University of California Press.

———— (1997). Immigrant families at risk: Factors that undermine chances for success. In A. Booth, A. C. Crouter, & N. Landale (Eds.), *Immigration and the family: Research and policy on U.S. immigrants* (pp. 79-87). Mahwah, NJ: Lawrence Erlbaum.

———— (1999). *Black identities.* New York, NY: Russell Sage Foundation.

Watson, J. (1974). Restaurants and remittances: Chinese emigrant workers in London. In G. M. Foster, & R. V. Kemper (Eds.), *Anthropologists in cities* (pp. 201-222). Boston, MA: Little, Brown & Co.

Westen, D. (1985). *Self and society: Narcissism, collectivism, and the development of morals.* Cambridge, England: Cambridge University Press.

Whiteley, W. H. (2004). A note on multilingualism. In E. Ardener (Ed.), *Social anthropology and language* (pp. 121-127). London, England: Routledge.

Williams, R. M., Jr. (1964). *Strangers next door: Ethnic relations in American communities.* Englewood Cliffs, NJ: Prentice Hall.

Wirth, L., (1938). Urbanism as a way of life. *American Journal of Sociology, 44*, 1-24.

Worthheimer, J. (1993). *A people divided: Judaism in contemporary America.* Hanover, NJ: Brandeis University Press.

Yancey, W. L., Ericksen, E. P., & Juliani, R. N. (1976). Emergent ethnicity: A review and reformulation. *American Sociological Review, 41*, 391-403.

Yang, P. Q. (1995). *Post-1965 immigration to the United States.* Westport, CT: Praeger.

Yinger, J. M. (1994). *Ethnicity: Source of strength? Source of conflict?* Albany, NY: University of New York.

Zhou, M. (1997). Growing up American: The challenge confronting immigrant children and children of immigrants. *Annual Review of Sociology, 23,* 63-74.

Zuidima, T. (2003). When the land is worn out: Eating corn with the ancestors. *World and I, 18*(6), 164. Retrieved from http://www.questia.com/read/1G1-105463784/when-the-land-is-worn-out-eating-corn-with-the-ancestors

# Index

African Americans, 19–20, 24, 25, 30, 31, 36, 39–40; 49, 53, 54, 57, 59, 60, 65, 77, 84, 86, 91, 103, 104, 105, 107, 109, 110, 112, 113, 115, 116, 121, 123, 128, 139
American dream, changes, 123–124
Americanization, child rearing practices, 125–129; socioeconomic mobility, 123–125
Ancestral reverence, 70–71; *See also* genealogy
Arabs, 55, 78, 85, 139
art, performance, 59–60; visual, 58–59
assimilation theory, 99–100

Bantus, 67, 72, 139
Belgians, 110, 125, 139
Black Muslims, 66, 108, 139
Bolivians, 67, 114, 124, 140
Bulgarians, 90, 139
Burmese, 127, 139

Chileans, 36, 54, 67, 88, 114, 140
Chinese, 36, 41, 51, 66, 86, 91, 124, 128, 139
collectivism, 4–5, ethnicity and, 94–97, 133–136
Congolese, 53, 64, 83, 90, 139
Cubans, 64, 140
Czechs, 57, 68, 139

DNA studies, 69, 136–137
Danes, 139
deindustrialization, effects on ethnic groups, 87–88
Dominicans, 140
Dutch, 72, 139,

English, 41, 65, 70, 73, 106, 113, 139

ethnicity, American attitudes toward, 104–111; collaborations around, 137–138; definition, 1–2; multiple backgrounds, 11–12; threats to, 129–130; urbanism 16–19
Europeans, 84–91; *See also* non-Europeans

families, benefits of ethnicity to, 93; child rearing, 125–129
Filipinos, 47, 108, 126, 139
Flemish, 110, 139
French, 33, 45, 57, 106, 110, 139
food, personal meanings of ethnic cuisine; 51–53; sociality of ethnic food, 53–54
freeway building, effects of, 119–123
genealogy, appreciation for sacrifice, 72–73; as identity, 71–72

Germans, 27, 29, 35–36, 41, 45, 52, 58, 59, 60, 64, 66, 69, 71, 83, 85, 89, 90, 106, 108, 110, 112, 116, 125, 139; German Russians, 35, 66, 109, 139
Greeks, 22, 46, 49, 55, 85, 89, 113, 139

Haitians, 140
healing practices, combining Western and folk medicine, 65–67; folk medicine, 67–68
healthcare, attitudes about Western medicine, 64–65
Hmong, 24, 31, 35, 45, 51, 59, 66, 70, 77, 83, 86, 86–87, 91, 109, 112, 113, 126, 128, 139
Hungarians, 139

Ibos, 109, 115, 139

immigration and migration, policies, 81–82; reasons for, 82–84
Indians, 40, 48, 54, 91, 108, 139
individualism, 4–5,
instrumentalism, 5–7
inter-ethnic tolerance, 111–117, 135–136
Irish, 12, 23, 26, 29, 37, 57, 60, 72, 75–76, 83, 85, 107, 109, 113, 115, 122, 124, 139
Italians, 25, 27, 28, 30, 34, 42, 46, 48, 49, 54, 55, 59, 60, 71, 83, 106, 108, 121, 122, 125, 139

Japanese, 51, 108, 139
Jews, 24, 27, 31, 34, 41, 43–44, 49, 52, 72, 78, 83, 105, 109, 116, 117, 126, 139

Kashubes, 70, 76, 89, 90, 107, 110, 128, 139
Koreans, 71, 139
Kurians, 65, 139

language, relearning, 36–37; retention 33–36
Latvians, 59, 139
Lithuanians, 27, 48, 139
Luxembourgers, 76, 139

Malinkes, 108, 139
Mbere, Kenya, 78, 139
melting pot metaphor, 99–102
Melungeons, study of, 136–137
Mexicans, 24, 26, 34, 40, 49, 55, 58, 65, 66, 78, 86, 88, 90, 91, 105, 109, 110, 113, 114, 115, 116, 124, 127, 140
migration. *See* immigration and migration
Milwaukee County, representativeness of, 17–19
Mina, South Togo, 83, 139
multiculturalism, 102–103

Nepalis, 47, 139
niches, establishing, 84–87, 96–97
non-Europeans, 84–91; *See also* Europeans

North American Indians, 19–20, 116, 140; Cherokees, 110, 140; Cree, 67, 140; Creeks, 104, 140; Ho Chunks, 34, 140; Lakota, 71, 140; Menominee, 16, 41, 105, 140; Ojibwe, 26, 36, 60, 76, 104, 109, 111, 116, 129, 140; Oneidas, 29, 34, 46, 58, 104, 111, 113, 140; Potawatomi, 54, 111, 140; Stockbridge Munsee, 30, 76, 111, 140
Norwegians, 30, 35, 41, 52, 58, 85, 89, 112, 139

organizations, creation of, 94–95; ethnic, 21–31; functions 22–31

Pakistanis, 86, 139
Palestinians, 28, 35, 41, 46, 54, 90, 107, 139
past, celebration of, 95–96
Peruvians, 140
pluralism theory, 101–102
Poles, 15, 16, 23, 29, 35, 42, 47, 57, 58, 85, 88, 90, 107, 112, 116, 122, 126, 127, 139
policies, anti-ethnic, 103–106; urban ethnic, 119–123
politics, advocacy for past homelands, 78–79; unequal access to power, 75–77
primoridalism, 5–7,
Puerto Ricans, 23, 34, 47, 48, 66, 77, 87, 109, 114, 122, 140

race, definition, 2–3,
relatives, support for, 40
religion, private consolidation with ethnicity, 46; public consolidation with ethnicity, 46–49. *See also* seculars
Russians, 44, 51, 53, 55, 65, 73, 83, 90, 107, 139

sacred cultures, 43
salad bowl metaphor, 102–103
Salvadorians, 23, 140
Scandinavians, 129
Scots, 29, 64, 71, 85, 108, 139

Scots Irish, 70, 71, 89, 106, 109, 125,
        139
seculars, 43–46
Serbians, 49, 55, 115, 139
Sikhs, 57
Slovaks, 40, 46, 57, 139
Slovenes, 26, 52, 67, 107, 112, 124, 139
Somalis, 78, 107, 139
Spaniards, 139
study methods, 1–15; participant
        checklist, 140; timeline, 140–141
support for past homelands, 40–41
Swedes, 73, 139
Swiss, 139
symbolic ethnicity, 101

Taiwanese, 35, 42, 59, 139
Turks, 90, 139

Urban Anthropology Inc., 1, 57, 137,
urban renewal, effects of, 119–123

Venezuelans, 27, 107, 140

Welsh, 59, 139
work ethics, 88–91

Yoruba, 60, 139

# About the Author

Jill Florence Lackey is an urban cultural anthropologist, specializing in urban ethnicity. She is the founder and principal investigator of Urban Anthropology Inc., a Milwaukee nonprofit organization that celebrates cultural diversity, trains young anthropologists, organizes ethnic events and newsletters, conducts ethnic research, and engages in urban problem solving. She taught research methods, cultural anthropology, and program evaluation at Marquette University for twelve years. Her publications include *Accountability in Social Services: The Culture of the Paper Program, Images of America: Milwaukee's Old South Side,* and numerous journal articles on ethnicity.